D0475324

AMERICA'S
WILDLIFE
HIDEAWAYS

NWF BOOKS

National Wildlife Federation

AMERICA'S
WILDLIFE
HIDEAWAYS

Copyright © 1989 National Wildlife Federation
All rights reserved. Reproduction of the whole or any part
of the contents without written permission is prohibited.

Library of Congress CIP data: page 237

CONTENTS

One of my most vivid outdoor memories is of a stop I made one day along Going-to-the-Sun Road. It was in August of 1981, and I had just attended my first meeting with the National Wildlife Federation's board of directors. The meeting was in Kalispell, Montana, very near Glacier National Park, where Going-to-the-Sun Road winds its way over the Continental Divide.

As I took a leisurely drive through the park, I spied grizzlies, moose, and a mule deer. The air was warm. Golden sunshine bathed the alpine meadow flowers and glistened on the rivulets. I quickly gave way to the temptation to stop my car and stretch out in the grass near one of the many crystal-clear brooks that traverse the meadows. Next I found myself taking off my shoes and dipping my toes in the stream. I caught my breath. This was a cold that makes you ache. The stream was flowing right off a glacier.

All my senses were alive with the wonder of the beauty and purity of Glacier National Park. I've had similar experiences in other natural places, from the Outer Banks in North Carolina to Denali National Park in Alaska.

Our parks, wildlife refuges, and wilderness areas—many run by federal and state governments, but some operated by private groups—make these experiences possible for all of us. The places described in *America's Wildlife Hideaways* are so widely dispersed around our country that most Americans are within driving distance of at least one of them.

But beyond being a vital link for Americans to their natural heritage, these places provide crucial habitat for our valuable fish and wildlife resources. Without the first, we will see rapid decline in the second. We can not afford to lose either.

Yearly, the National Wildlife Federation urges Congress to appropriate adequate funding to properly maintain national parks and refuges, and to properly manage the wildlife inhabitants. The Federation consistently lobbies for or supports legislation that proposes setting aside additional areas of wild lands in our parks and refuge systems. All the while, our natural resource experts keep vigilant eyes on which areas are considered for designation, to be certain we are protecting the richest and most valuable habitats.

As you read about the spectacular wildlife hideaways in America, remember that they are your hideaways as well, and offer experiences found nowhere else. Enjoy them!

Jay D. Hair

President, National Wildlife Federation

THE PACIFIC NORTHWEST

Sometimes the land in Alaska is like a song. It soars to the horizon with a wild harmony of mountains, forests, tundra, and rivers. Denali National Park is like that. But add Alaska's wildlife—the moose, foxes, wolves, grizzlies, and caribou—and the song becomes a symphony.

"Freedom prevails," wildlife biologist Adolf Murie wrote about Denali decades ago. "The foxes are free to dig burrows where they will; to hunt ptarmigan, ground squirrels and mice as the spirit moves; and they share in the ownership of the blueberry and crowberry patches. The grizzlies wander over their ancestral home unmolested; dig roots and ground squirrels, graze grass, and harvest berries according to whatever menu appeals to them."

Murie spent 25 summers in Denali researching wildlife. At times his young daughter joined him, once crawling over a rise with her father to watch a family of wolves play by its den near the Toklat River.

"Our task is to perpetuate this freedom and purity of nature, this ebb and flow of life," Murie wrote, "first by insuring ample park boundaries so that the region is large enough to maintain the natural relationships, and secondly, to hold man's intrusions to the minimum."

On the recommendations of Murie and others, Mt. McKinley National Park, established in 1917, was enlarged to almost six million acres (roughly the size of Massachusetts) and renamed Denali National Park and Preserve in 1980. A single dirt road winds 90 miles into the park as it dips into spruce forests, crosses braided rivers, and climbs over tundra slopes that stretch as far as the eye can see. To reduce traffic and therefore prevent scaring wildlife away from the road, the National Park Service strictly limits private vehicles. Instead, visitors travel by yellow shuttle buses that depart from the visitor center at half hour intervals starting at 6:00 a.m.

By that early hour, a line of bleary-eyed visitors from all over the world is stepping aboard the bus to begin a journey of a lifetime. As the bus climbs out of spruce forest and into tundra, a man in the back yells, "Moose." The bus driver brakes and 40 people snap awake. "Where?"

Standing among the spruce about 100 feet away are three moose—a mother and twin calves. The passengers crowd to the side of the bus, slide the windows down, stick out their cameras and shoot. The moose stare back, then browse on willow branches. Where the mother goes, the calves go, staying close by her side. The bus driver explains that the forest isn't as safe as it looks, for grizzly bears are out there,

Preceding page: Viewing Mt. McKinley without its cap of clouds is an iffy proposition, despite nearly 24 hours of summer daylight. Summer is a good time for visitors to look for caribou *(above)*.

FAIRBANKS

ANCHORAGE

Hoary marmots (*left*) spend much of the summer gathering grass to line their burrows in preparation for their winter hibernation. Denali's Dall sheep (*below*) seem to know that passengers on the park's tour buses wield nothing more threatening than cameras.

somewhere, waiting for the opportunity to attack a moose calf. Rare is the grizzly that will battle a full grown moose protecting her young, because one kick from a moose is as dangerous as a swipe from a bear. The moose may be twice as tall and weigh twice as much. But should a moose calf stray from its mother, the bear will attack it without hesitation.

Across the tundra the bus rolls, while the passengers talk and watch for wildlife. Suddenly a woman yells, "Stop, driver. I see Dall sheep." A thousand feet above the road a band of Dall sheep grazes on a tundra shoulder of a mountain. A dozen of them, ewes and lambs, move nimbly about the steep contours. They are the only wild white species of sheep in the world. Roughly 2,500 live in Denali National Park, out of 70,000 in Alaska.

While feeding, one or two ewes always keep their heads up, watching for danger—wolves, grizzlies, and red foxes. Should trouble appear the sheep race for the cliffs and scamper along narrow ledges where other animals cannot follow. For now, though, they are relaxed. Two lambs chase each other across the tundra, springing as they run. One circles back to where the rest have bedded down, bounds over the back of its mother and resumes its chase.

In the miles that follow the passengers see a red fox, a golden eagle, and 20 caribou. Shy at first, they now sound like students on a high school field trip.

"There's a grizzly bear," an elderly woman calls out a few miles down the road. The bus stops.

"Where?" others ask.

"Out there on the tundra, by that pond."

"That's just a rock," they answer.

"No," she says, "it's a grizzly bear."

Everyone takes a closer look. "Sorry, it's a rock."

"It can't be," the elderly woman says, almost pleading, "it's too big to be a rock."

Farther into the park the woman gets her wish, and more, as a family of four bears—a mother and three cubs—ambles across the road in front of the bus.

At the heart of the park, rising through gray clouds, is 20,320-foot Mt. McKinley, the highest mountain in North America. Often obscured by overcast skies, the peak is nevertheless the centerpiece of the park. Years ago, native Alaskans called it Denali, The High One, the name adopted by the park while the mountain itself (to the dismay of nearly every Alaskan) retains the name of a U.S. president who never visited Alaska or, for that matter, admired mountains.

Despite a large number of preying grizzlies, moose in Denali have prospered. A cow moose is fiercely protective of her young and doesn't hesitate to take on a threatening grizzly *(below)* when necessary. But when the next crop of calves is born, it's the yearling who's sent packing *(left)*.

At the end of the road at Wonder Lake the bus stops and everyone gets out for a stroll. Some walk along the shore, others spread out over the tundra, getting down gently on hands and knees to admire up close the constellations of small wildflowers. A loon calls, the lake ripples, and sunshine dances on the water.

Denali has been called a "subarctic Serengeti," the diversity and sheer numbers of its wildlife reminiscent of the famous area in Africa. Perhaps that's an exaggeration, but after seeing bands of Dall sheep, herds of caribou, and families of moose, bears, loons, and marmots all moving through this wild land, the exaggeration no doubt can be forgiven.

During the summer, Dall sheep ewes and lambs find the precipitous ledges of Denali's mountainous regions *(below)* a comfortable place to relax. Rams either remain solitary or form their own small bands. Pudgy arctic ground squirrels *(bottom right)* stock up on seeds while the weather is still balmy.

Feathered to the tips of its toes, the willow ptarmigan is well suited to its harsh northern habitat. Perhaps that's why Alaskans chose it as their state bird. A male willow ptarmigan, its red "eyebrows" flashing, shares a perch atop a spruce tree *(below)* with a small white-crowned sparrow.

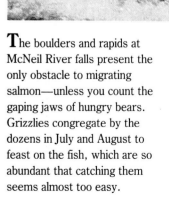

"S hoo!" The bear stops, lifts his giant head and stares at 10 people only 20 feet away. His claws scrape on the rocks. He lumbers forward, and again veteran bear biologist Larry Aumiller motions with his hand and softly says "Shoo."

The hulking, 800-pound Alaskan brown bear stops and stares, waves his nose in the air, then saunters back down to the river to catch salmon.

"When you've got 10 people and 40 bears in the same place at the same time," says Aumiller, "things like this happen. The bears are curious, that's all. They know we're here and they check on us from time to time." And so it is at Alaska's McNeil River State Game Sanctuary, where dozens of bears go about the amazing business of catching salmon, and a handful of fortunate people from around the world go about the amazing business of watching bears. Alaskan writer/photographer Cecil Rhode first described the McNeil phenomenon in *National Geographic* in 1954, but declined to specify its exact location for fear of endangering the bears. Sixteen years later the sanctuary was established. Today, so many people want to see the bears that the state chooses visitors by lottery. Your chances of getting picked may be less than 1 in 10, but that way people don't outnumber the bears.

"Last year we had 109 bears on the river," says Aumiller, "and most of them we knew by name—Groucho, White, Anita, Teddy, Luigi, McBride, Dallas, Dalhart. It makes it easier to identify them. Each has a distinct personality. Some are mellow, others are hyper. I suppose Teddy isn't a good name, though. It implies something cuddly, and that's one thing these bears are not."

Aumiller has been the caretaker at McNeil River for 14 summers, the past two with Colleen Matt, his wife and assistant and an excellent bear observer herself. Larry and Colleen were married at McNeil. For gifts they received fine art prints of bears, towels embroidered with bears, drinking mugs covered with bears, even joke books about bears.

Every day in July and August, Larry and Colleen take 10 visitors along a two-mile trail from their camp at McNeil Cove to an overlook next to a waterfall on McNeil River. Gathered in pools beneath the falls are thousands of salmon, which in turn attract dozens of bears. The visitors have all applied, but failed, to get into McNeil before. Now they've finally made it—a pharmacist from Chicago, a couple from New York, a writer from California (who's tried five times to have his name chosen for the trip to McNeil), two college students from

The boulders and rapids at McNeil River falls present the only obstacle to migrating salmon—unless you count the gaping jaws of hungry bears. Grizzlies congregate by the dozens in July and August to feast on the fish, which are so abundant that catching them seems almost too easy.

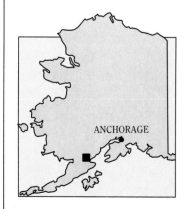

ANCHORAGE

Switzerland, and several professional photographers. They set up their tripods and telephoto lenses and begin to capture the action: two young bears battling waist deep in the water over a fishing hole, an old bear catching salmon between his forepaws, a mother nursing three cubs in the grass nearby.

After about six hours at the river (and 70 rolls of film for each photographer), Larry and Colleen take their visitors back to camp. "That's when the experience hits them," Colleen says. "Walking back they have the time to think about what they've seen. They erupt with stories and talk into the night and make new friends.

"That's what makes McNeil so special," she adds, taking a sip from her brown bear coffee mug. "It reminds people that a world without bears would be a sorry place."

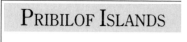

The Pribilof Islands emerge from the Bering Sea as though seen in a dream—dark, basaltic shores shrouded in summer fog and splashed by waves. A certain defiance pervades them, and a poetry as well. Their steep cliffs climb hundreds of feet above the sea, then level off onto an emerald plateau of summer grasses and wildflowers. To lie among that greenery at clifftop and peer over the edge is to behold a wondrous sight, for the rocky ledges below are alive with birds.

Only 25 feet away might be a tufted puffin or 20 thick-billed murres. And beyond them are thousands more, some calling through the salty air, some preening themselves, others swooping downward over the sea.

The murres crowd together on narrow ledges, side by side and breast to breast, swinging their heads to survey the vertical world around them. Their call is half purr, half growl, and when hundreds call at once—as they often do—they sound like frantic Wall Street stockbrokers in the closing minutes of the trading day. They build no nests, laying their eggs right on the cliffs, a precarious place. Yet the eggs are safe. They are shaped elliptically, not like chicken eggs, and roll in

Murres by the millions flock to nesting cliffs at St. Paul each summer to hatch their chicks. Adults *(far left)* jump into the sea with ease, but some chicks, unaware of the perils of high-rise living, may leap into the sea prematurely. To prevent their young from getting an ill-fated jump on mother nature, adults often place themselves between chicks and the cliff edge. Northern fur seals and tufted puffins also congregate at St. Paul Island to strut their stuff for prospective mates. The puffins *(left)* acquire their distinctive tufts and bright bill coverings for the occasion. The seals just add extra fat.

Surprisingly, murre eggs don't require a nest *(above)*. Their pear shape and pointy end make the speckled eggs roll in tight circles instead of off the cliff.

Black-legged kittiwakes *(right)* must nestle their eggs in the safety of seaweed and grasses cemented together with mud. A young kittiwake *(top, right)* is ready to leave its mother and take to the air about six weeks after hatching. Kittiwakes spend most of their lives at sea, eating fish and crustaceans.

tight circles instead of straight off the edge of the cliffs.

Interspersed with the murres are kittiwakes, small gulls whose name is a phonetic derivation of their high-pitched call, *kittiwake, kittiwake*. Returning from the sea, they wheel in the air and fly straight toward the cliffs, stalling at the last minute to land on their nests, which are no more than bits of twigs and mud plastered onto a narrow, rocky ledge. In some places the cliffs are so crowded that whenever one bird lands it forces another to take off.

A dozen birders from New Jersey move along the cliff-top, each with a pair of binoculars, a few with cameras. Like most visitors to the Pribilofs, they've flown thousands of miles and depleted their savings to get here. Never mind that it's foggy, windy and cold, for these are the Pribilof Islands, a veritable North American mecca for anyone and everyone interested in birds. Many of the places on the Pribilofs where visitors go to see and photograph wildlife are part of the Alaska Maritime National Wildlife Refuge.

Last night the visitors slept in a rustic hotel in the hamlet of St. Paul, and then—still a bit bleary-eyed from the four hour time change and jet lag—traveled a few miles by bus this morning to the cliffs. But from the moment they stepped outside and saw the birds, the jet lag was forgotten. "This is everything I had hoped for," says a woman named Helen, thumbing through her well-worn bird book. "Now, if only I could find a least auklet."

"Helen," another woman calls from 50 feet away. "Come quickly." Helen creeps over and, looking down, sees two crested auklets, six parakeet auklets, and one least auklet, all perched on the same large rock. "Good grief, three species of auklets on one rock?" she gasps. "Sure enough," answers the group leader, an ornithology professor. With unabashed flare Helen pulls out her life list, a record of every species of bird she's observed in North America, and checks off the least auklet. "Three hundred and eighty," she says with evident satisfaction. "Not bad."

Far below the auklets is a boulder covered with pigeon guillemots, birds as black as coal and highlighted with brilliant red legs and feet and white patches on their wings. Their faint, high-pitched whistles can barely be heard over the crashing surf. Rather than nesting on cliff ledges, they lay their eggs in crevices among the boulders and talus.

Tufted puffins also use crevices, but each couple prefers to dig a burrow four to six feet deep at the top of a cliff where sod and grass meet bedrock. At the back of this burrow the female lays a single egg. While one puffin feeds out at sea, its mate stands guard at the burrow entrance, largely unconcerned about the humans photographing it from 25 feet away.

With its orange feet and legs, black body, white face, red ring around the eye, and soft yellow tufts over the ears, the tufted puffin is hard to miss. But the hallmark of this bird, and of the horned puffin as well, is its brightly colored beak. A child with crayons could hardly draw something more flamboyant, yet the puffin beak is critically important during courtship and mating. A puffin with something less couldn't attract a mate.

After waiting an hour above the puffin burrow, Helen watches the other puffin return from sea and waddle about with its mate. The two preen each other's necks and rub beaks, and Helen takes 30 photographs with her 400mm lens. All things considered, she's in birder heaven.

While the murres growl, the kittiwakes call and the guillemots whistle, the puffins seldom utter a sound, waddling about with an almost comical lack of grace. Agility on land is hardly a forte among seabirds. Being heavy-bodied, they also pay a price in the air, flapping their wings furiously to stay aloft. Gliding is a luxury these animals cannot afford. Yet puffins, murres, guillemots, and auklets can dive to depths of more than 100 feet in water, actually "flying" underwater in pursuit of fish. Think of their versatility: rare are the animals that can dive, fly, and walk, no matter how ungainly they may appear to humans.

From the lush grasses on top of the cliffs emerges an arctic fox. Thin to the point of looking emaciated, it climbs into a narrow draw and suddenly appears along the cliffs. At once hundreds of birds screech and take to the air in a great winged cloud. The fox is slate gray, with light, almost translucent, ears. Its eyes are hazel and penetrating. The fox creeps out a narrow ledge until it's balanced on three legs, straining to reach a kittiwake egg only five feet away. The cliff drops 100 feet to the sea. The parents scream overhead. The fox tries one more step, teeters, and backs away. He may find more accessible eggs, and perhaps chicks as well.

How did arctic foxes get to the Pribilofs? They probably arrived during an exceptionally cold winter long ago when ice formed over the eastern Bering Sea, connecting the Pribilofs with the Alaska mainland. No people lived on the islands then. And when people did come, beginning a couple of centuries ago, they came unwillingly, as slaves.

In the summer of 1786, while delegates in Philadelphia worked on the Constitution of the United States, a Russian fur

giving birth to a new generation. The once rugged rocks have been worn smooth beneath the seals' shuffling flippers. The shiny black pups cry for mothers that somehow pick them out among the others, while the 600-pound bulls stand guard like sultans over their territories and females.

Male fur seals subscribe to a "more is better" credo, so it's not unusual for a bull from one territory to steal a female from another. While his neighbor isn't looking, a bull dashes over, grabs a 100-pound female by the nape of her neck, and begins dragging her. The defending bull charges over and tries to tug the female back, while nearby pups scamper away lest they get crushed in the commotion.

Watching wide-eyed from behind a large wooden blind are Helen and her friends. Having visited the bird cliffs and then returned to St. Paul for hot soup and sandwiches, they'll spend their afternoon at this seal rookery. Helen wrinkles her nose at the stench of hundreds of fur seals. "It smells like a locker room," she says under her breath. "You'll get used to it," a researcher assures her.

Most of the seals are down by the water, but one young bull sits on the rocks only 20 feet from the blind, nursing wounds he sustained in a fight days ago. His eyes are dark, his whiskers blond, his ears small and curled into tight rolls. He waves his nose in the air as he detects people, then bellows and growls. His fur consists of a soft inner layer and a coarse outer layer, together totaling more than 300,000 hairs per square inch. Thick, glossy, impenetrable to water, and insulating, this fur enables seals to survive in cold water, yet it also brought about their near extinction.

Today, the number of fur seals is strong again. Pribilofians who once lived on a fur-based economy are moving toward a fishing-based economy. In 1988 the settlement of St. George, with only 200 or so people, was recognized for its economic survival and for its bicentennial celebration. It became the smallest community ever to win the National Civic League's All American City Award. The Aleuts smile with pride, for it isn't easy living on a small island in a cold, windy, foggy sea. But they do it well.

After an afternoon at the seal rookery, Helen and her friends board the bus back to St. Paul where they'll spend the night sharing impressions and preparing for their short flight to St. George tomorrow. Someone notices that above the rear-view mirror the Aleut bus driver has taped a sign showing a puffin smoking a cigarette with a red line slashed through it and the words, "NO PUFFIN." Everyone laughs.

merchant named Gerassim Pribilof became lost in the Bering Sea. He discovered the islands that today bear his name, islands covered with seabirds and millions of northern fur seals. For Pribilof and other Russians, it proved to be a gold mine. But for the fur seals, it became a holocaust.

The Russians captured and indentured the Aleuts, the native people of the Aleutian Islands, and shipped them to the Pribilof Islands to harvest furs. The first year, 40,000 seals were killed, and in the decades that followed millions more died as American, British, and Japanese furriers joined in the slaughter. Twice the fur seals nearly slipped into extinction, and twice they recovered.

In 1867, Alaska, including the Pribilofs, was bought by the United States. In time the Russians went home, but not the Aleuts. They still live on the largest two islands, St. Paul and St. George (44 and 35 square miles, respectively). The other three islands (less than a square mile each) remain uninhabited. Both St. Paul and St. George have a small town of the same name with a simple wooden Russian Orthodox church in the center. Although the family names are Russian (Krukoff, Rukovishnikoff, Kochutin) the faces are Aleut.

And the northern fur seals? Things have improved significantly since the 1972 Marine Mammal Protection Act. Each summer more than a million fur seals cover the rocky beaches of the Pribilofs, grunting, barking, scratching, and

One day in March the sunshine melts the air, wild grasses turn green, and meadowlarks sing from fenceposts. Ranchers gather in a cozy little cafe in Burns, the largest town around, to sip coffee and talk in upbeat tones. It's been a long, cold winter and things are finally warming up. Spring has come to eastern Oregon.

This is high desert country where sagebrush hills roll to the horizon and rimrock mesas level off in a way that's distinctly western. Buttes bear the names Rattlesnake, Coyote, and Saddle, and the land has a sweep that carries your eye and imagination far away. Remove a few things—cars, paved roads, electric coffeepots—and it could be the 1890s.

Up on Steens Mountain, snow melts into creeks that tumble down Blitzen Valley into Malheur Lake, a huge marsh and centerpiece of the 185,000-acre Malheur National Wildlife Refuge. Looming as an island of water in the middle of the Pacific migratory bird flyway, Malheur is an avian rest stop. In the course of a year you could find 300 species of birds and 58 species of mammals here.

"What I like about Malheur is its diversity," says Gary Ivey, a wildlife biologist at the refuge for six years. "There's always something different here—birds heading north, birds heading south, or those staying for the winter or summer."

Wildlife watchers can best see the show, from trumpeter swans and shovelers to roosting turkeys and tree swallows, by making frequent stops on a leisurely auto-tour route through this land of lake and sagebrush. In fact, refuge staffers suggest staying *in* your car, using it as an observation and photographic blind.

For organized groups with more time, the Malheur Field Station hosts college classes, high school field trips, teacher workshops, and a program for senior citizens. "This is where the classroom comes to you," says director Lucile Housley. "People learn more here than they do in a month back home. And they have a lot of fun."

On the agenda one night is a lecture by Carrol "C.D." Littlefield, a local legend who's spent 22 years at Malheur studying sandhill cranes. Before an eager audience he discusses the majestic gray birds with bright red foreheads, and how and why they leap into the air while flapping their wings, kicking their feet, and calling wildly. Once thought to be solely a courtship dance, the behavior has since been observed in cranes of all ages and at all times of the year, performed for any number of reasons.

At the end of his talk Littlefield mentions the 5,000 to

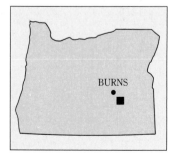

BURNS

Male red-winged blackbirds *(far left)* arrive at Malheur on the heels of the spring thaw to stake out their nesting territories before the females show up. In the early 1980s, meltwater from heavy snows flooded Malheur, Harney, and Mud lakes, creating one huge lake. This large lake, dotted with marshy island hideaways, attracts hundreds of stately white pelicans *(below)* who come here in the summer to nest.

The beacon-red foreheads of greater sandhill cranes aren't the only feature that sets them apart. The birds' eye-catching stature—they weigh as much as 14 pounds and stand up to 4 feet tall at maturity—marks them as the largest form of sandhill crane and makes them easy to spot on the marshy expanses at Malheur refuge.

7,000 cranes that spent a few days last fall in a nearby field. A woman asks, "How do you count all those cranes?" Littlefield points his finger at each person in the room, one after another, and slowly counts, "One, two, three, four. . . ."

By late March clouds of snow geese are rising off the hayed meadows, stroking their white and black wings through the blue Oregon sky. Circling in loose formation, by sheer numbers and movement they create their own wind. White-fronted geese join them, calling with a loud *kah-lah-aluck . . . kah-lah-aluck*, flying and circling until, at a time intuitively sensed within this old fraternity of fliers, the geese turn north toward their summer nesting grounds in Canada and Alaska. Come autumn, they will return to rest and feed en route to southern wintering grounds.

As the geese depart, and as Malheur, Mud, and Harney lakes swell with meltwater, other birds arrive to raise their young—white pelicans, western grebes, American avocets, and long-billed curlews, to name a few.

A sixth-grade teacher from Portland who brings her class to Malheur every spring is back again. An hour before dawn on the first morning at the field station, she tells her students to be ready to leave in 30 minutes. "This was supposed to be fun," mumbles one, "but it's more like boot camp." They pile into cars and take off. Their objective: sage grouse.

Every spring at dawn in the hidden corners of Malheur, male sage grouse gather at mating grounds called leks and, like knights of yore, do battle for the company of females. You couldn't ask for a wilder courtship display. Strutting with tails raised peacock style, they emit a loud *pop, pop, pop* by inflating and deflating air sacs in their throats. The students watch wide-eyed from cars parked on a dusty road in the middle of the lek. That night at the field station they hold a contest to see who can do the best imitation of a sage grouse. The creative winner had taped balloons to his neck and tied a lamp shade around his waist.

The next morning they visit Buena Vista Ponds, a highlight on the tour route because the water attracts wildlife all year. Shining iridescent in the sun, a male red-winged blackbird grasps a cattail and surveys the marsh. Splaying his wings, he lifts his head and begins his gurgling song, *konk-la-reee, konk-la-reee*, ending with a trill. Then he calls in a quick *chack, chack* to let the world know this particular piece of marsh belongs to him. Another blackbird responds *chack, chack* and lands on a nearby cattail. The first blackbird chases him away. *Chack, chack.* So there. It's all part of defending

Attack or attract? Either purpose might be served when the sandhill crane produces its attention-getting threat display *(below)*. This move and other aggressive behavior often appear in the cranes' courtship dance.

one's territory—serious business among male blackbirds who must find a mate and raise a family by fall. Yellowheaded blackbirds do the same, but with even greater aggression, singing with a rasp and buzz and calling with a *croak, croak, croak*. Add it to the red-winged blackbird's repertoire and the marsh becomes a cacophony of trilling, rasping, and croaking.

The students waste no time working on their blackbird imitations but no one conjures up a song even remotely as beautiful as the red-winged male's.

Unmindful of the blackbirds, a great blue heron stands motionless on the far shore, waiting for a meal to swim by. One does. In a flash the heron comes up with a small fish, impaled on the end of its dagger-like beak. The heron flips the fish into the air, catches and swallows it, all in one fluid motion. The whole affair takes 10 seconds before he is back to a frozen position again, waiting.

Barn swallows dart over the pond, snatching insects off the surface, changing direction instantly without missing a beat. Coots call from behind the reeds while shovelers, mallards, and ruddy ducks paddle the lapis lazuli water. Tundra and trumpeter swans add an elegance to the busy pond as they swim with heads held high. Only the trumpeter nests at Malheur, while the tundra swan continues north to the Arctic.

Streaking across the rolling hills at speeds unrivaled by any other North American land animal, the pronghorn seems a fitting match for the windblown desert uplands ringing Malheur.

Every so often a coyote slips through the shoreline grasses in search of anything edible. Lean, wary, always on the move, it is the ultimate opportunist. But perhaps the most amazing mammal in Oregon's high desert is the pronghorn antelope, drinking the wind as it dashes over sagebrush hills. Only one animal can run faster: the African cheetah.

Many years ago biologist Arthur S. Einarsen was driving near Malheur when a pronghorn buck began to race him. "He gradually increased his gait," Einarsen wrote, "and with a tremendous burst of speed flattened out so that he appeared as lean and low as a greyhound. Then he turned toward us at about a 45 degree angle and disappeared in front of the car, to reappear on our left. He had gained enough to cross our course as the speedometer registered 61 m.p.h. When he reached a rounded knoll about 600 feet away he stood snorting in graceful silhouette against the sky as though enjoying the satisfaction of beating us in a fair race."

A century ago pronghorns numbered 30 to 50 million across the American West. Today, after suffering the same sorry fate as the American bison, about 800,000 exist. Seeing them bound through the sagebrush of Malheur imparts a sense of promise to the place.

Not only pronghorns suffered. Swans, egrets, herons, and grebes were killed for their feathers, which society had decided looked better on women's hats than on the birds themselves. Market hunters killed the birds by the thousands, collected their plumes, and left the bodies to rot. In a few years the great egrets of eastern Oregon were gone, and the other species nearly so.

President Theodore Roosevelt ended the slaughter when he established Malheur National Wildlife Refuge in 1908. Soon the birds began to recover, especially after 1935 when the refuge was enlarged to include the vitally important watershed in Blitzen Valley.

The sixth-grade students talk about this during their visit. They talk about wildlife and conservation and why Malheur and places like it are so important. Before beginning the drive home, the teacher asks them to share their feelings about the wildlife refuge.

From one: "I enjoyed imitating the birds. It helped me understand why they act the way they do."

From another boy: "I think it's neat to have a place like this in Oregon."

A shy girl in the back quietly says: "I think it's impossible to sing like a red-winged blackbird, but I wish I could."

For 362 days of the year, Bowerman Basin looks like an undistinguished mud flat. But from April 23 to 25, an amazing array of migrating birds enters the north end of Grays Harbor and turns the setting into a wildlife watcher's dream.

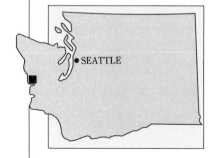

eregrine falcon!" A dozen heads turn toward the sky; eager college biology students raise their binoculars and focus. Meanwhile the falcon folds its wings and plummets earthward into Bowerman Basin, a tidal flat at the northern end of Grays Harbor on the Washington coast.

Then sandpipers—20,000 of them—lift into the air and collect into a synchronized cloud, turning left, then right, their wings shimmering each time they change direction. The falcon flashes past, singles out an isolated sandpiper, grabs it and flies away, all in one fluid motion.

"Wow! Did you see that?" asks a student. "That wasn't a bird, it was a bullet," responds another. The sandpipers circle twice more, then land in the basin. The rising tide forces them to huddle up the shore closer and closer to the students. Suddenly they take flight again, moving together as though choreographed, the air whooshing behind them.

The students stand wide-eyed. Once the spectacle is over, they erupt with questions. "How can they fly like that?" "It's like they've got radar." "Do they ever collide?" The man with the answers is Steven Herman, ornithology professor at Evergreen State College in nearby Olympia. "They collide sometimes," he says, "but not very often."

Herman and his students stand in rubber boots and wool sweaters on this windy, cloudy April day. Despite the cold, they are warmed by the sight of one of the most impressive

Diminutive dunlins and
western sandpipers find safety
in numbers at Grays Harbor
(left). Large flocks effectively
deter predators, since spotting
a single target within such a
checkerboard pattern is difficult.

yearly concentrations of shorebirds in all of North America.

"At high tide during the peak of migration, a half million shorebirds are driven into the basin," notes Doug Plummer, who has photographed the scene. "With the right tidal conditions, the rising waters of Grays Harbor will bring the shorebirds practically to your feet."

Plummer recalls one memorable spring day when he and several other birdwatchers thrilled to the sight of thousands of roosting shorebirds. "Rain squalls alternated with bright sun, and the shorebirds would take to the air en masse upon the approach of a falcon."

Like clockwork, as many as one million migrating shorebirds may be found at Grays Harbor at this time of year, about half of which gather in Bowerman Basin every April 23 to 25. Up to 90 percent are western sandpipers; the rest are dunlins, dowitchers, red knots, and 19 other species on their way to summer breeding grounds in Canada and Alaska.

Why Bowerman Basin? Because the basin is slightly higher than the rest of Grays Harbor and thus remains exposed longer between high tides. That affords the birds more time and area to feed. "You've heard about the swallows at Capistrano?" asks Herman. "I think this phenomenon makes that pale by comparison."

Perhaps a little pride imbues his voice, for Herman discovered this spectacle in 1979 while on a birding trip to Grays Harbor. When he arrived, he couldn't believe his eyes. Like other well-trained birders, he counted the birds in estimated groups of 100 and multiplied from there. One thousand. Ten thousand. One hundred thousand. "I had simply never seen that many birds in one place in all my life and I kept wondering why other people hadn't reported these numbers and why this place wasn't known around the world." The reason: previous bird census takers had visited the basin on the 15th and 30th of each month and had missed the peak migration. Yes, a few casual birders had happened upon the basin during the peak, but they hadn't realized its significance.

Herman notified several conservation organizations and the U.S. Fish & Wildlife Service, and after nearly a decade of debate and compromise the 1,800-acre Grays Harbor National Wildlife Refuge was created in August, 1988, to protect the birds of Bowerman Basin and the surrounding area. A visitor center, boardwalk, and viewing points will soon be built to accommodate the hundreds of people who come each April to watch the great collections of shorebirds moving in their magical, mysterious ways.

By imitating a feeding elk, photographer Tom Leeson was able to avoid alarming this ruffed grouse and thus capture its spring territorial display on the Olympic peninsula *(above)*.

Temperatures rarely dip below freezing or climb above 80° F in temperate Olympic rainforests *(right)*. Sword ferns and big-leafed maples thrive on the 145 inches of rain a year that drench these green, thick-canopied sanctuaries.

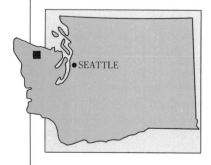

SEATTLE

Ozette, Quinault, Queets, Bogachiel, Quillayute, Hoh—even the names are different on the Olympic peninsula. Anchored in isolation on the Washington coast, the Olympic Mountains form the heart of a world where culture and ecology seem to have taken a less familiar turn.

The Pacific Ocean lies to the west, the Strait of Juan de Fuca to the north, and Puget Sound to the east. Seattle, the biggest city in the Pacific Northwest, lies across Puget Sound less than 50 miles away but might as well be 10 times that far. Some people on the peninsula have never been there, and don't intend to go.

Give Seattlites half a chance, however, and thousands will escape from the city to enjoy the wilderness in Olympic National Park, the centerpiece of the peninsula. Over thousands of years, glaciers have carved out peaks and valleys, creating a lush but craggy landscape that contains three worlds in one. Where else can you hike on trails past alpine wildflowers and up to rugged mountain summits, stroll through a rain forest of 200-foot-high trees, and walk along a breathtaking seashore, all in one park?

Here white phlox and yellow lomatium cover the alpine meadows, heather and lilies spread over the open slopes. Black bears lumber through the brush. Roosevelt elk and Columbian black-tailed deer follow the rivers, then spread out into the dimly lit forest. And the forest ends where great bluffs meet the sea and the calls of gulls and oystercatchers mingle with the sound of pounding surf. At low tide you can explore the tidepools, with careful eyes sorting out objects that first look like rocks or gaudy flowers, but in fact are sea creatures.

The Olympic peninsula has long been a favorite haunt of Tom and Pat Leeson, husband and wife photographers formerly from Port Angeles but now living in Vancouver, Washington. "Live in a place and snoop around it long enough and you get to know it real well. The Olympic peninsula is like a big back yard for us," says Pat. "One year in March we found a ruffed grouse in an alder bottom. Tom tried to approach without disturbing it, but couldn't. A herd of elk came by and the grouse did nothing, so Tom acted like an elk and pretended to browse around as he approached the grouse. Eventually he got within arm's reach of it. The next four years we returned to the same spot at the same time and there would be the same ruffed grouse, waiting like an old friend. It would stand beneath a spruce tree protected from the rain while Tom took pictures from out in the open, soaked to the bone."

Walking through the colorful wildflowers and early morning mists along Olympic's Hurricane Ridge *(right)*, a hiker might encounter a black-tailed deer fawn *(above)*, an Olympic marmot, or one of many other mammals that inhabit this northeast section of the park.

People on the west side of the Olympic peninsula say it's a nice place to live if you're an umbrella. It can rain nonstop for a month. The Hoh and Queets valleys get 120 to 150 inches a year—more rain than any place else in the contiguous United States. Under the thick forest canopy, the temperature seldom drops below freezing. The result is a temperate rain forest where Sitka spruces often become 200 to 300 feet high and 15 to 25 feet in circumference.

A certain majesty permeates this forest. A dozen inventions of green surround you—emerald, olive, grass, jade, apple, beryl, chartreuse. Living plants take up nearly every bit of space. The silence lingers until broken by the flitting of a winter wren, the cry of a bald eagle, the quick flight of colorful harlequin ducks and mergansers off gurgling rivers.

Because of its isolation, the Olympic peninsula contains animals that probably exist only in the Olympics: two varieties of rainbow trout that live in Lake Crescent, several species of wildflowers (Flett's violet and Piper's bellflower are two examples), a species of marmot, and subspecies of mole, chipmunk, weasel, and pocket gopher. On the other hand, other species that inhabit the Cascades and the Rockies have never

reached the isolated Olympics. They include the lynx, grizzly, wolverine, bighorn sheep, and pika.

Unfortunately, the most famous animal in the Olympic Mountains, the mountain goat, is also the most destructive. For many years the fragile alpine vegetation in the Olympics existed without mountain goats or any other large herbivore. Then in the 1920s a dozen were introduced. Now more than 1,000 goats are trampling and eating plants, some of them rare, in Olympic National Park. "An early explorer named the highest peak Mt. Olympus after the ancient Greek 'Home of the Gods,' " wrote Charles Bergman in *Smithsonian.* "But putting mountain goats here turned out to be like putting rototillers in heaven."

"We plan to remove every goat from the high country," says Chuck Janda, chief ranger of Olympic National Park. "It's a huge task, but everyone agrees it has to be done. We live-trap them using nets, helicopters, and medication to prevent trauma, then ship them to places where they occur naturally in Idaho, Montana, and other parts of Washington," Janda explains. "It costs about $750 per goat and gets dangerous for rangers in helicopters hovering next to cliffs. Last year we captured 80 goats and lost only seven."

It's not easy explaining the goat issue, especially to children. A ranger named Jill does it while leading them on a scheduled hike for students on Hurricane Ridge, a popular summer destination in the northern part of the park. Hundreds of avalanche lilies and blue lupine brush their pant legs as they walk along, talking about goats and fragile plants and how the two don't mix. Suddenly Jill stops and kneels next to what she thinks is cougar scat. Everyone huddles around to see. "Cougars live up here," she says, "but I've never seen one."

Suddenly a loud whistle pierces the wind. The kids pop to attention and look around. "A marmot," says Jill. "Let's find him." The kids run ahead and spot a marmot perched on a rock, alertly surveying his world. Jill explains, "He's a sentinel, standing guard while others in his colony feed. When danger approaches, he whistles and they run for their burrows."

"Does he think we're dangerous?" asks a young boy.

"Not as dangerous as a cougar, coyote, or eagle. Those are the guys he needs to worry about." The students relax in an alpine meadow with the sun on their backs and a gentle breeze in their hair. "You know," a young boy finally says, "if I were a marmot up here I wouldn't worry about a darn thing."

"Really?" says Jill. "And you know where you'd end up? In cougar scat." They laugh and head down the trail.

Wings folded, legs lowered and taloned toes spread wide, a bald eagle hurtles out of the gray January sky of northwest Washington State, calling as it lands on a gravel bar to pull a spawned salmon from the riffling waters of the Skagit River. Another eagle flies down and displaces the first. Then another, and another, each lifting its head and calling in a high-pitched cry.

Watching from a highway pullout about 200 feet away is Libby Mills, steward at the Nature Conservancy's Skagit River Bald Eagle Preserve. "I really like the smell of dead fish," she says, chuckling. But her eyes reveal her seriousness. "It means the river is healthy, that salmon are spawning and dying, and that eagles are here feeding on them. It's the way it's supposed to be."

She kicks her feet together to keep them warm. Binoculars hang around her neck, a wool hat covering her head. Three eagles perch in a cottonwood nearby, their white heads and dark bodies a regal addition to the leafless tree. Half a dozen other eagles feed on salmon on the gravel bar below. Mills notes their numbers and interactions, plus the weather and time. It's her job. Last night she gave a slide presentation to a group of school children. And today is eagle census day.

"I've been doing this for seven winters," she says. "You'd think I'd get tired of it, but I don't." She mentions the times she has seen 35 eagles soaring on a January afternoon, or watched dozens huddled around a gravel bar in the rain.

Every winter eagles gather along the frigid, smooth-running Skagit to feed on salmon which have died after their spawning run up river. "The more salmon, the more eagles," says Mills. The eagles must cope not only with unreliable salmon runs, but also with logging in forests where they roost at night and with increased human activity along the river.

All this concerns Mills. "On sunny winter weekends there might be 75 boats on the river, some with fishermen, others with eagle watchers, and dozens of cars on the highway looking for eagles. I talk to every person I can and ask them all to be respectful. Most of them are."

Bald eagles, however, are only half the winter wildlife spectacle along the Skagit. Down on the flats where the river meanders past farms and fields and enters Puget Sound, great numbers of snow geese, tundra swans, and trumpeter swans gather against the cold. "I've seen harriers, peregrine falcons, and snowy owls out there, too," says Mills. "I suppose that's why I love the Skagit so much," she adds with a smile. "It's my home. And it's wild."

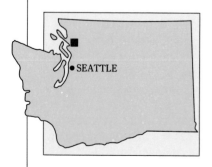

Winter is a season of plenty at Skagit. Bald eagles *(left)* find a bountiful supply of spawned salmon (fish make up 90 percent of the eagles' diet), and snow geese *(below)* stop to refuel on leftover grain in nearby fields.

THE WEST

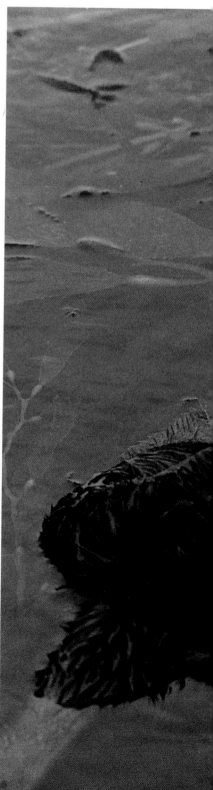

Preceding page: A golden blanket of lupines covers the cliff tops at Pt. Reyes. The lupines' long roots help keep shifting soil in check. Egrets and herons nest nearby, while on the shore, tide pools fill with an array of fascinating creatures.

Point Reyes is a green-meadowed, pine-forested peninsula an hour north of San Francisco—and moving ever farther. Separated from the mainland by the San Andreas fault, Pt. Reyes is moving north at a rate of two inches per year. That doesn't prevent its broad beaches and rocky cliffs from being one of San Franciscans' favorite places to watch wildlife. Its glory is creatures of the edge of the water—marine birds and mammals.

On a spring day, the mudflats at Bolinas Lagoon are thronged with western sandpipers, marbled godwits, and long-billed dowitchers on their way to arctic Canada and Alaska. The flocks wheel restlessly over the lagoon, then settle like windblown leaves to feed. Up a side canyon is a heron rookery, and in April you can climb the hillside and look down into treetop nests to watch young herons and egrets croak for their parents to return with fish from the lagoon.

From December to February, Pt. Reyes lighthouse is a good spot from which to watch gray whales migrate south toward their calving lagoons in Baja California. The whales move close to shore here, and without binoculars you can see them breach, exhale a steamlike cloud of breath, and then arc slowly back into the water, the huge flukes hanging ponderously in air just before the whales dive. On a sunny January day, a visitor may take delight in several whales an hour.

On their annual migration from Baja California to the frigid Arctic, gray whales pass so near the Pt. Reyes lighthouse that watchers on shore easily can view them. The ponderous mammals swim in pairs like this mother and youngster *(far left)* or in small groups. Whales can spout moisture-laden air 10 feet high. In the big kelp beds off Pt. Reyes peninsula, sea otters *(below)* live a seeming life of leisure. The weasel family's largest members, bewhiskered otters spend much time paddling on their backs. To keep from drifting out to open sea while napping, they anchor themselves with strands of the seaweed.

Chartered boats bring visitors close enough to look at the murres, cormorants, and other birds on the Farallons' rugged landscape *(below)*. Granite ledges *(right)* serve as breeding grounds for two types of sea lions: large, cork-colored Stellers and smaller, darker California sea lions.

The nearby Farallon Islands, about 30 miles west of San Francisco and part of the San Francisco Bay National Wildlife Refuge, are a cluster of weathered granite rocks jutting out of the sea, the highest only 340 feet above the water. They contain the largest seabird colony in the continental U.S. In the spring, 300,000 puffins, murres, cormorants, auklets, and gulls nest on these rocky outposts. At night, the air is manic with the weird laughing cries of auklets. By day, you hear the barking of sea lions, the bugling of elephant seals, and the crash of 15-foot waves. The noise of life is dizzying.

From December through February, hundreds of elephant seals come ashore on the Farallons. Huge 14-foot-long bulls endure bloody combat to stake out territories on the beaches. When they prop themselves up on their flippers, the bulls stand seven or eight feet high. They throw back their heads and their trunklike noses wobble over their faces as they challenge rivals with glugging noises that sound like water being emptied from an enormous jug. But they are serious. Their leathery necks and faces are often deeply scarred from years of breeding battles. Around each beachmaster, 20 or 30 cows may loll, nursing their newborn calves. After the females wean their calves, they mate and then go back to sea.

The only humans allowed ashore on the islands are usually researchers from the Pt. Reyes Bird Observatory. In summer and autumn, the Oceanic Society in San Francisco runs day-long boat excursions around the South Farallons for wildlife watchers. They offer views of the rich bird life, including frigatebirds, shearwaters, and seldom-seen albatrosses. On these tours, voyagers may sometimes get glimpses of blue, minke, or humpback whales. Rare sights indeed, but all the more surprising when you can look over your shoulder and see one of the nation's largest cities just behind you.

Their slender necks extended in choreographed harmony, western grebes *(right)* skitter across the water. The grebes vie to impress potential mates in their walk-on-water courtship dance. Impressive numbers of migrating grebes, stately tundra swans *(top, right),* ducks, and geese funnel into a narrow corridor that empties into the Klamath Basin, a vast expanse of lake and marsh astride the California-Oregon border.

YREKA

The Klamath Basin is one of the few places where you can still see wildlife in astonishing numbers. On a November morning you can stand at the edge of Tule Lake while 40,000 snow geese swirl overhead, alternately darkening the sky with their numbers and dazzling the eye with the reflection of sunlight on their white wings. The noise of their wingbeats alone sounds like a jet lifting off an airport runway, and their collective whooping rings through the air like the crowd at a Saturday afternoon football game. It is electrifying and inspiring. And when you consider that these birds have come all the way to California from the Soviet and Canadian arctic, you get a sense of the curve of the earth and the sweep of wind and time. You feel the tug of continents and the pull of seas—rhythms older and more sweeping than anything in human experience.

The Klamath Basin, a vast expanse of lake and marsh, sits astride the California-Oregon border. It is a desert setting and the low hills rising from the basin are covered with the gray-green of sagebrush. But snowcapped mountains encircle the basin, and the combination of lake and mountain peak brings to mind the glacial epochs of geological time. Majestic Mt. Shasta, a volcanic peak covered year round with snow, looks down on the lakes. Lonely, brooding, always playing tricks with clouds and sunlight, it is a photographer's dream. Some people even think the peak serves as a kind of visual landmark, guiding birds as they fly down from the north.

In the fall, at the peak of the migration season, more than a million waterfowl may be drawn to the Klamath Basin. The basin lies at a crossroads in the migration routes of dozens of species of birds. Ducks, geese, and swans flying from the Arctic to wintering grounds in California and Mexico are squeezed into a narrow corridor between the Cascade range on the west and the Great Basin desert on the east.

The traffic is sometimes astonishing. On a single autumn day, 130,000 snow and Ross' geese, 100,000 white-fronted geese, and 50,000 cackling Canada geese have been counted. In addition, huge numbers of mallards, wigeons, gadwalls, and teal abound. "It's probably the best place in Oregon to see large numbers of species," says Ralph Opp of the Oregon Department of Fish and Wildlife.

A quarter million pintail ducks have descended on the marshes in a single fall. The drakes' white breasts stand out in the low winter sunlight as they preen on the banks of the sloughs and lakes. When feeding in the shallow water, they dip their heads to uproot submerged bulbs and roots, and their delicate pointed tail feathers point skyward. By December and January, the pintails have gone, replaced by mallards and wigeons that mingle on the open water at night, swimming and stirring up the water to try to keep the ice from closing in on them and freezing them to death.

By late February, they are starting to pair. A single hen rises off the water and swoops over the marshes, followed closely by seven or eight drakes. The drake that wins the hen will accompany her north to Alaska or to the Canadian pothole country as she returns to breed, quite likely on the very pond where she hatched. The pintail's courtship flight is one of the classic scenes of American wetlands, often celebrated in duck stamps and paintings. It is a reminder of the restless energy of life and of the eternal patterns of flight and seasons.

Winter is also the time of eagles at Klamath. The basin has one of the largest winter concentrations of bald eagles on the continent, with more than 900 eagles counted in 1988. They roost in tall firs on the ridges to the south and forage for food, including ducks and geese that freeze into the lake ice on cold winter nights. On a February morning, you may see as many as 300 eagles lift off a night roost within an hour after sunrise. They flock to the fields farmers have flooded for rodent control and stand hunch-shouldered and grim, looking for a drowned vole or a winter-weakened duck. As the Klamath's lakes ice over, many of the ducks and geese move south.

But the spring and summer months see astonishing numbers of birds return. Pintails, gadwalls, mallards, redheads, and ruddy ducks all breed in these secluded marshes. Each spring, at least 10,000 tundra swans pass through on their way to breeding grounds in the north. Great passages of phalaropes, dowitchers, and grebes fill the skies. Such sights suggest that the world is rich with possibility and purpose.

In the spring and summer, white pelicans swim in stately clusters, while greater sandhill cranes come to earth with a loud northwind bugling. Tall, straight-legged, gray as storm clouds, they move like ermine-robed princes through the grain fields. Western grebes perform their strange walk-on-water courtship dances in which, after a bout of head bobbing, a couple skitters across the water on their webbed feet, their wings stretched back, necks extended.

Some biologists estimate that 80 percent of the waterfowl using the Pacific flyway pass through this basin on the spring and fall migrations. All this bird life attracted market hunters around the turn of the century. In 1903, hunting camps along lower Klamath Lake alone sent 120 tons of ducks

and geese to San Francisco markets and hundreds of bales of plumes and skins of grebes and terns to manufacturers of women's hats in New York.

To protect the birds, President Theodore Roosevelt set aside the first of the basin's refuges, on Lower Klamath Lake, in 1908. Five others have been added over the years, including Upper Klamath, Tule Lake, Klamath Forest, and Clear Lake National Wildlife Refuges. Today some of the best places to see vast numbers of birds are the auto-tour routes on the Lower Klamath and Tule Lake units. Upper Klamath has a canoe trail where water birds can be seen.

Most of the basin's lakes and marshlands have been drained and converted into farmlands. Only 48 of the original 300 square miles of surface water remain, and most of that can be drained or refilled to adjust to the birds' nesting and feeding needs. All the lakes are edged with dikes and levees. Under contract with the Fish and Wildlife Service, about 10 percent of the refuge lands outside the dikes are farmed under terms which leave a third of the grain in the fields for the wildlife to feed on. In the fall, the snow geese loaf in the afternoons in dense white masses, surrounded by the safety of the lake water, looking like distant ice floes; but in the mornings they fly up in great clouds, swoop over the dikes, and feed greedily in the grain fields. By the time winter ice impels them south, the stubble in the fields has been trampled flat by the broad feet of feeding geese.

It is a heavily managed landscape. But it boasts a kind of abundance we seldom see. The air is crisp, the sky clear, and snow powders the distant mountain ridges. A flock of 20,000 mallards may fly up from a grain field, circle noisily, and settle invisibly back into the stubble. You sit at the edges of these marshes and listen to the squeaks of wigeons, the crank of mallards, the whoop of snow geese, the whistles of pintails. You gaze up at the snowy peak of Mt. Shasta and think this must have been the way things used to be long, long ago.

Creating a flurry of feathers on a winter's afternoon, a northern harrier hawk snatches a duck *(above)* that has been trapped by ice. Visitors to Klamath can view wildlife year-round, but autumn is the basin's glory. Great numbers of waterfowl descend, and the air fairly echoes with the honking and whooping of hundreds and hundreds of snow geese *(right)*.

It's not what I expected of the Mojave desert: all the way up the rocky trail into the Queen Mountains, the air fairly quivers from the distant thunder of artillery fire. Thirty miles to the north, across the Morongo Valley, charcoal gray puffs of smoke rise, marking the site of some apprentice warfare being conducted by United States Marines. As I approach the ridge, the whistle of a jet builds and then suddenly an F-18 sweeps low over the ridge with a deafening roar.

Such a rumble and clash seem much out of place here in the desert's eternal stillness and ancient patience. The conflict between the quiet of the desert and the noise of civilization is jarring, disconcerting. But just ahead, over the jumbled granite of the ridge and through the scrawny creosote bushes, something wondrous comes into view: the deep leafy green of palm trees. A desert oasis.

Another half mile down the trail to the canyon stand dozens of 30-foot tall California fan palms, broad-leafed and drooping, tropically luxuriant and wholly unexpected in the desert. Some have black charred trunks, the result of fire. But others wear coverings of dried fronds all the way to the ground, great brown hula skirts 12 feet thick. One rattles mercilessly when I bump into it, no doubt scaring away any creature deaf enough not to have already heard my footfalls. I clamber down white granite boulders into a world of cottonwood shade and bunchgrass carpeting.

In the Mojave desert, these oases are the best places to see wildlife, for in summer, desert creatures repair to these rare water sources every few days to drink. Even though it is November, I'm hoping especially to see some desert bighorn sheep. According to staff biologist Bob Moon, the impressive bighorns are "the single most requested animal" of visitors who journey to Joshua Tree National Monument, a half-million acres of southern California desert. Perhaps 200 bighorns live on the monument grounds.

I sit down on a smooth granite boulder in the shade of a fan palm and listen to the water trickling quietly through a series of clear, calm pools. Water striders loaf on the surface. Bees drink at the damp edges of a sandy beach. Cattails nod. A pair of rock wrens, small cinnamon brown creatures with soft white throats, alight on a neighboring boulder. A red-tailed hawk soars along the canyon walls. Tracks in the sand tell of skunks, snakes, cottontail rabbits, coyotes, and lizards. But no bighorn. Bob Moon had told me it is unlikely that I would see them down here in November.

All through summer, the trail to this oasis is closed to the

To Bible-toting pioneers, the outstretched arms of these trees resembled the prophet Joshua at prayer—thus the name, Joshua tree *(above)*. Clumps of the shaggy trees dominate the western half of the monument grounds. A favorite of Saturday morning cartoon fans, the roadrunner *(right)* zips along real-life desert sands at speeds up to 30 mph, thanks to its powerful legs.

LOS ANGELES

public because the bighorns drink here daily and humans can easily spook them and keep them from drinking. In summer months, most of the springs in the higher country dry out, and sheep stay close to the few remaining water holes.

"There are some bands of sheep that hang out around particular water sources all summer," Moon had explained earlier. Not all of the water holes are closed to the public, so summer visitors who ask rangers where to see the sheep and who are willing to hike and wait patiently usually succeed in seeing bands of bighorns.

With cold weather, the wildlife disperses. The reptiles and insects go underground. Many of the rodents do, too. "Bighorn sheep are still out there," explained Moon. "But you have a tougher time spotting them because they're no longer congregating around the water." And in the fall, the rams have

begun to assemble harems of ewes and move them into higher country. The breeding areas are remote, the boulder-strewn terrain hard for a human to cross. Moon has heard the clash of horns as rams butt each other in mating combat. But, he said, "I've never seen it."

Higher up, the rocks are so fractured and tumbled that they look as if some mountain god upset a vast basket of stones. They are virtually the camel color of a sheep. Even if a ram were up there, I would probably miss him unless he waved a red flag and shouted. Rangers here suggest you look for them standing out against the ridge lines.

Looking for wildlife at Joshua Tree is almost two separate experiences. The monument spreads over two distinct desert provinces. At higher elevations the Mojave holds its juniper and pinyon pines, scrub oak, and the strange Joshua trees, yucca trees whose spreading branches suggested to pioneers the biblical Joshua beckoning them farther west. At lower elevations the Colorado desert, with its sweep of desert playas, is dotted with cholla cactus and ocotillo and is dissected by drywashes strewn with the ghostly figures of smoke trees.

In the Mojave, elusive mountain lions and bobcats stalk the rocky ledges. In the Colorado, you delight in smaller things: on a summer night you can go out with a flashlight and look for kangaroo rats and mice, sidewinders and scorpions, creatures that seek the cool of underground burrows by day, when surface temperatures can rise well above 120° F. On the soft sand dunes, you may unexpectedly sink into the burrows of the kangaroo rats, desert creatures that are about the size of grapefruits. In the dim light, everything appears silvery blue, and a vole might hurtle into a clump of brittlebush like a golf ball hit into the rough.

Or by day you may see fringe-toed lizards, specialized reptiles whose flattened heads and scaled toes allow them literally to swim under the sand's surface to escape predators. Large, leathery chuckwallas sun on the dark desert varnish of rocks. Brilliant emerald green collared lizards dash across the roads. Horned toads and rosy boas abound, along with whiptail lizards and rattlesnakes—a generous and varied complement of desert reptiles.

What people yearn most to see after the bighorn, said Moon, are not the reptiles but the roadrunners. These strange birds are ubiquitous, both in the Mojave and the Colorado, skulking along looking for lizards and snakes to feed upon. If you interrupt one, it will stop, lift its long tail and erect the crest on its head at the same time, and cock its head so that

A desert seems forboding to many humans, but the visitor who takes time to stroll can delight in the pink blossoms of a beavertail cactus *(left)* or the frantic dash of an emerald green collared lizard *(below)*. Most cacti lie dormant for months, unfolding their blossoms only when rain finally comes. It is usually most rewarding to see Joshua Tree by foot early or late in the day. The collared lizard, for instance, is most commonly spied on spring and early summer mornings.

you see the bright turquoise lores behind the eye. Then it will lower both the head and tail, extend its neck, and run low to the ground, like Groucho Marx. Along the monument's paved roads, roadrunners may run ahead of a slow-moving car for a hundred yards or more.

Seeing any of this requires some sense of what you're looking for and where it may be. And since few of us live in the desert, few of us go out there with that familiarity. But at Joshua Tree, you can ask a park ranger how best to see such things as bighorn and roadrunner, kangaroo rat or chuckwalla, and come up with some success. Kit foxes, you'll be told, are likely to be seen at night along the dry washes of the Pinto Basin. Fringe-toed lizards and kangaroo rats frequent the sand dunes. Gray foxes may be seen in the rocks near the Mojave oases, agilely scrambling over and around boulders in pursuit of lizards they feed upon. Bighorn sheep are found in the higher, better-watered parts of the park.

So I keep scanning the ridges. And sure enough, on a distant ridge, something shines in the sun. As I look through the binoculars it moves, revealing itself as the white rump of a browsing sheep. The animal leaps a few rocks with remarkable agility, then slowly folds its legs and sits like a sphinx. Judging from its small, goatlike horns, it is either a female or a young ram. There must be others with it, but I can't see them.

I listen intently for the sound of horns crashing together. But all I hear is the abiding quiet of the desert. The muttering artillery fire and screaming jets of the morning seem very far removed from here.

An overcast day finds a prairie falcon perched high above the Snake River. Like other birds of prey, the falcon can move far and fast while hunting. The world's densest concentration of nesting raptors lives here: northern harriers, red-tailed hawks, golden eagles, and several varieties of owls. But since predators usually are solitary and dispersed, it takes a little more time and effort for the visitor to appreciate them.

The world's densest concentration of nesting birds of prey may not, at first glance, be much to look at. There are no clouds of birds. "The less trained observer can go down there and not see anything," says Mike Kochert, a Bureau of Land Management biologist who has worked at Idaho's Snake River Birds of Prey Area for more than 16 years. "But right over his head may be a nesting prairie falcon." And from one spot, Kochert can see 15 different prairie falcon nest sites at once. That is something a person can do nowhere else.

Five percent of the world's prairie falcons nest here. So do large numbers of northern harriers, ferruginous hawks, red-tailed hawks, kestrels, and golden eagles and a respectable number of Swainson's hawks, turkey vultures, great horned owls, long-eared owls, short-eared owls, screech owls, and burrowing owls. It is, by all odds, the best place to study raptors in the nation, perhaps the best in the world.

Viewing raptors is more demanding than other kinds of wildlife watching. Some raptors often sit still and seem to do nothing—they perch on a rock staring out at the air—or else they move fast and far in the act of hunting. That makes them different from grazing mammals that move slowly across the prairie or shorebirds that cluster at the edge of a tidal flat. Predators tend to be solitary, so the viewer loses the striking patterns of massed creatures. Instead, you look for the speed and precision of the raptors' stoop or the impressive agility of rapid flight. Or you look for the more abstract patterns of ecological relationships. You think about how the soil sprouts the seed which feeds the prey—which feeds the hawk.

The unusual concentration of raptors at Snake River is, to some degree, due to geology. A combination of factors produced good nesting sites and high numbers of prey. On the north side of the Snake River here, the soil is a deep loam made of windblown ash from volcanic eruptions in the Cascades thousands of years ago. The north bank's soft soil affords easy burrowing for Townsend's ground squirrels, which live here in vast numbers. The soil also grows abundant sage, winterfat, and other plants that feed immense rodent and jackrabbit populations. All those voles, squirrels, rabbits, and kangaroo rats are what attracts the hawks, owls, and eagles.

The second oddity of geology is the high rugged basalt cliffs that brood over the deep canyon of the Snake River. All those cliffs afford a great density of nesting and roosting sites. It is the combination of abundant food and nesting sites that seems to concentrate the raptors here.

A young long-eared owl *(left)* is among the raptors drawn by good nesting sites and high numbers of prey. The abundant sage and winterfat plants attract ground squirrels and rabbits, and they in turn attract predators.

Photographer William Mullins saw prairie falcons the hard way. Mullins was hanging from a rope photographing some chicks while his partner held his safety rope. When the mother prairie falcon attacked Mullins' partner, he let go of the rope—and Mullins nearly fell off the cliff. The average wildlife-watcher, however, need not endure the hardships that photographers and scientists do.

At Dedication Point, the canyon is about one-half mile wide and the cliffs 700 feet high. The Snake River flows green and quiet below, with just a faint rush from a distant rapid audible over the whistle of the wind. Perhaps the best way to see the canyon is to take a day-long rafting trip into the gorge with one of the several outfitters in the Boise area who offer them. For the adventurous, a jeep track runs along the canyon floor.

The riparian corridor glimmers green and willowy, full in spring of the song of warblers and tanagers. Behind the willows, slopes of grass and sage rise toward the chocolate colored cliffs. On a summer day, the canyon floor remains cool and quiet, and the morning air fills with swallows and swifts, flitting gracefully.

But summer is not the best time to see the raptors. In summer heat, the ground squirrels go underground, and most of the falcons and hawks which feed on them move away from the area and begin the nomadic movements that take them north into the mountains, or east to Kansas, or south to Mexico. Summer residents include a few golden eagles (they feed chiefly on the jackrabbits available all year) and red-tailed hawks (which feed on reptiles as well as rodents) and lots of ravens and kestrels. But in summer the raptor species with star billing are fewer in number and not so easily seen.

Experienced wildlife-watchers know the best time to visit is in March, when the raptors have returned. Red-tailed hawks and prairie falcons begin arriving late in January, and ferruginous hawks in early March. By March, the prairie falcons are courting. They perform spectacular aerial dances, soaring hundreds of feet aloft, then diving suddenly, braking just below the canyon rim and wheeling back into space. Prairie falcons are intolerant of eagles, and when an eagle soars through the canyon, a half dozen different prairie falcons may, each in turn, give chase.

April is again a quiet month, for the hawks are brooding. But in May, the nests are full of fledging young, and parents fly regularly to bring food back to the nests. Eagles and falcons may be seen coming and going, passing nests in which their young stand up and scream at them for food. With binoculars or a sighting scope you can see the cranky, half-feathered chicks teeter as they demand their meals.

You can take a perch yourself out in the sagebrush away from the canyon to watch falcons hunt. In spring, the ground squirrels are so abundant that you see them scurrying everywhere. So do the falcons, which swoop powerfully down to catch them. With patience and good binoculars you may follow a falcon as it soars over the desert searching for food. It stops to hover, like a hummingbird, in midair. The dive that follows is spectacular, swift and unerring. The bird folds its wings back and falls like an arrow. The moment of impact is likely to be lost in the sage—perhaps you'll see only a wisp of dust and the edge of wings as the bird spreads them over its dying victim. A moment later, the falcon lifts off heavily, carrying its prize back to the nest. The act seems small and far away, but it is the essence of what knits an unusual population of falcons to this unusual place.

Perhaps the best way to see the canyon is by canoe in early spring, floating down the green and willowy corridor of the Snake River. Slopes of grass and sage rise toward cliffs of 700 feet. With patience and good binoculars, a visitor can see such raptors as the young ferruginous hawks *(left)*.

In this land of widestretched spaces, a hiker seems dwarfed by mountains and mesas and an expanse of sagebrush. Though separated by 70 miles, Hart and Sheldon share similar habitat, and both are favorite haunts for backpackers and for pronghorns.

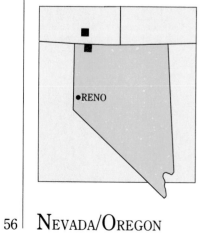

RENO

Prairie grass and sagebrush grow abundantly on the rolling tablelands, creating good settings for pronghorns to bear and feed their young. By summer's end, the young pronghorns will be dashing on the plains as exuberantly as their parents. Visitors to Sheldon may see a carefully managed herd of wild horses that shares the open prairie with jackrabbits, pronghorns, and other wild animals.

Standing at Sheldon or Hart Mountain wildlife refuge, you may be conscious of the whistling of the wind and the silent circling of ravens. For this is the realm of high desert sage: yawning open spaces, mysterious cloud shadows, a subtlety of color. At Sheldon's Bald Mountain summit in Nevada, you look down over a broad expanse of sage and alkaline lake and mesa. The distant lands fade to blue and grey until you are not sure whether you are seeing land or sky or mirage. It is a land that might be inhabited by spirits.

The real inhabitants are many and varied: green-tailed towhees, sage thrashers, black-throated sparrows, golden eagles, and prairie falcons. This is a good place to watch the strange mating dances of sage grouse hens. Mule deer, coyotes, jackrabbits, and ground squirrels abound here.

But the main attraction is the pronghorn—high-spirited, in motion much of the time, moving to some appointment over the horizon. You see them in bands of three or four or fifty. Near Sheldon's Catnip Mountain, more than 100 may be in view on a September morning. As you approach, they sprint off, the white hairs around their rumps everted into a kind of flag that flashes the desert sun as they run, sometimes as fast as 60 miles per hour.

Now and then you may come upon pronghorns when they are resting, and a single buck may stand like a sentinel, staring hard at some distant mirage. A pronghorn's vision is said to equal that of a human using an eight power telescope. If so, it is vision made for these spaces that stretch forever.

In late summer, when mating is about to begin, the bucks get restless and may suddenly jump from this motionless position to the right or left, for no apparent reason. Or they may dash off across the prairie. A pronghorn just seems to love to move like the wind.

Hart Mountain in Oregon is higher and better watered than Sheldon. At the refuge's western edge, mountains rise like huge purplish battlements over the lush Warner Valley, with its hayfields and large alkaline lakes. The lakes draw vast numbers of migrating waterfowl, and bald eagles winter there. Up on the high ridges, about 500 bighorn sheep roam.

The tablelands that roll east from this escarpment are good spring and summer range. There, pronghorns give birth to and nurse their young through summer. In May and June, fawns seem to be everywhere, popping up from a patch of sagebrush or gamboling exuberantly across the flatlands. But temperatures can drop to 20 below zero in winter, and then most of the pronghorn move to Sheldon's lower elevations, where they subsist on sagebrush.

The adults have by then lost their horns. They may mass into bands of several hundred. As the winter winds blow, flecking their fur with snow and whiting out the distant ridges, the pronghorns stand blinking out the cold and pawing up bits of sagebrush. Perhaps they are dreaming of summer months when the sky is clear and they are again running with the wind.

An aerial view *(above, right)* shows the U-shape of Molokini Islet, a sunken crater where fish and other marine life tend to congregate. Scuba divers relish Molokini's clear blue water for sights like the school of lemon butterfly fish *(right)*.

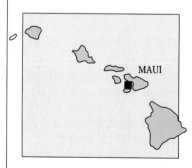

MAUI

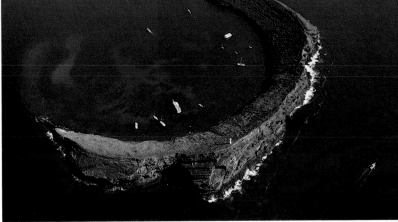

Among Hawaii's manifold pleasures, the least heralded may be its wildlife. Yet in the deep mountain forests are rare endemic honeycreepers, a dozen species of brilliant red, yellow, or green birds that you can see nowhere else. On the islands' northern shores, spectacular frigatebirds and albatrosses, long winged wanderers of the open sea, soar along the steep cliffs.

But the best of it is in the water. Coral reefs off the island of Maui offer dozens of excellent places to dive and snorkel. Honoloa Bay, a marine preserve on the north shore, has deep canyons and a wide variety of fish. At La Perouse Bay, a preserve on the south shore, snorkelers marvel at elegant yellow and black Moorish idols, their long fins streaming like pennants behind them, and at parrotfish of powdery blue-green hues, as big as pigs, biting off mouthfuls of coral and spitting out puffs of sand. Strange trumpetfish, long fat broomsticks in the water, eye you warily as you swim over them.

The colors are dazzling. A young yellowtail wrasse is as brilliant a red as you'll see in nature, with clownish white spots outlined in black. Surgeonfish seem to have electric orange neon lights on their sides. Engrossed in these beauties, you find yourself swimming after them over coral hills and canyons, like the hapless victim of some watery enchantment.

One of the easiest ways to see Hawaii's underwater wonders is to take a snorkeling or scuba diving tour boat to Molokini Islet, a partially submerged volcanic crater a few miles off Maui's southern coast.

Dozens of boats go out every morning from Maalaea, Kihei, Lahaina and other harbors. The boats anchor in the crater and the operators chum the water, throwing bait fish to attract fish. They arrive in dazzling schools: silvery rudderfish come up to stare at you, and bright yellow butterfly fish beg for handouts. You may see sharks here: one boat captain said he sees them on about 80 percent of his visits, but they never seem threatening as long as people leave them alone. That's not hard, since the water is so clear at Molokini that the shark you see may be 170 feet away. You may also see an enormous manta ray, 20 feet across, gliding dark and gray through the water like a water-borne cloud.

Maui is exceptional in the Hawaiian chain because it is the best island from which to look for whales. From December through May, humpback whales swim from Alaska to give birth to calves in the warm deepwater channels to the east and south of Maui. You can watch them from the shore. You're likely to see in the distance a cloud of white spray burst from

the blue water. And if you watch through binoculars or a spotting scope, you may see the whale breach again and again, like a child trying to splash water from a pool. A single whale may leap entirely out of the water, then crash like a falling tree into an explosion of foam and spray that you can hear miles away.

You also can take tour boats out to see the whales up close, within a hundred feet if you are lucky. Along the way, you may encounter pods of pilot whales or porpoises surfing the bow waves of the boat.

Humpback whales are an endangered species. It is illegal to harrass them by jumping into the water to swim after them, as some people nevertheless do in the Au Au channel out of Lahaina. It is also dangerous. Deborah Glockner, who has studied these whales for 15 years and spent much time watch-

ing them, reports that whales sometimes breach as a result of violent underwater combat between males, who follow a cow in hopes of being the handiest male about when she is ready to breed. Under water, the noise of whales smashing into one another sounds like the combat between linemen in a professional football game.

The whales usually shy away from humans. The tour boats that take visitors out to see them stay a respectful distance and do not pursue the whales when they move away.

Still, you may encounter whales in the water. You may be several hundred yards from shore, swimming off a sailboat when, with luck, you may see a dark shape deep beneath you and hear the haunting warble of whale song through the water. Then you may notice the white fins splayed like oars out to

Off Maui, several species of whales roam the sea, but the most commonly seen are the humpbacks *(below and left)*. Watching these giant mammals dive or breach is an unequalled treat. The humpback whales swim here from Alaska to give birth to their calves in the warm channels. Charter boats full of spectators may come within viewing distance of the whales. Closer approaches might disturb these endangered behemoths.

the sides. A cow may be snoozing beneath you, her calf resting above her, chin cradled on her back. The mother must surface every 10 to 15 minutes to breathe, and the calf must come up for air even more often.

A cow and her calf are likely to move away as soon as humans enter the water. But on one outing, I had the privilege of swimming with a tolerant mother and her calf. The calf—a 15-foot behemoth looking primitive and armored—slowly rose from her mother below. She appeared a dappled yellow-green in the refracted light beneath the waves. She swam playful, lazy circles around me, 20 feet away, rolling slowly over and over as she turned, blowing bubbles. One enormous questioning eye fixed upon me and I felt very much that I was the wildlife being watched.

THE SOUTHWEST

Preceding page: Saguaro cacti dominate the landscape in this section of the Sonoran Desert. Saguaros can reach 150 years in age, 50 feet in height, and a massive 8 tons in weight. These prickly giants are home to a multitude of desert animals.

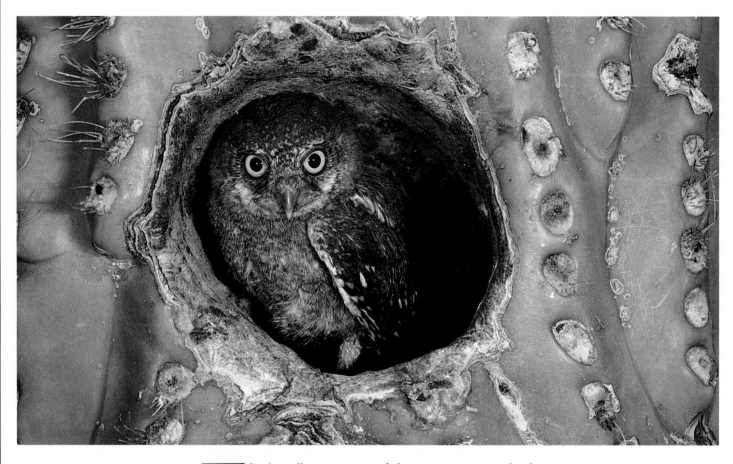

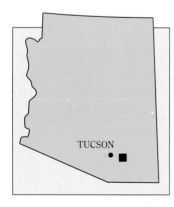

TUCSON

The brooding presence of the saguaro cactus dominates all else on the silent, arid hills of this desert land on the outskirts of Tucson. The saguaro, up to 50 feet tall and weighing several tons, towers over the rolling terrain. Its spiny green arms seem to order "Halt!" or "Welcome, you may pass," or to shrug in lordly indifference. Indians believed some of the saguaros were ancestors who, wandering about, had become affixed to the ground.

What seems at first a barren, desolate expanse of sand and rocky earth soon reveals itself otherwise to visitors who take the time to look around Saguaro National Monument. The saguaro (pronounced *sa-WHAR-o*) works as the pivot of a complex ecosystem containing many animals. A visitor can observe all the desert's fascinations from roads and trails throughout the monument, although, for the adventurous, walking cross-country is likely to bring more intimate awareness. Those who do get off the trails should be *very* careful to

The gilded flicker, undaunted by the saguaro's sharp thorns, excavates a nesting hole *(below)* which later is used by a succession of tenants, including elf owls *(far left)* and other birds. Perched here among the saguaro's May-blooming flowers, the red-tailed hawk *(left)* uses the cactus' branching arms to cradle its bulky nest.

avoid touching or backing into cactus; one variety is known colloquially as the "horse crippler."

Walking up close to the saguaro, you can see flickers and Gila woodpeckers. They nest in hollows they industriously excavate among the spines in the great cactus' trunk. In self-defense, the saguaro lines the holes with a sticky secretion that hardens to such a tough layer that the shell of the nest can survive even after the cactus has died. Here eggs are laid and fledglings grow up, protected against outside temperatures that can soar to more than 100° F. The plant's insulation cools the nest by as much as 20 degrees.

When the woodpeckers finish nesting, other birds, themselves unequipped to hollow out cavities, move in and raise their families. Screech and elf owls, purple martins, flycatchers, and kestrels all come. A single saguaro can be a veritable apartment house, its inhabitants protected by the plant's spines from predatory animals.

One night in late May or early June the saguaro opens its crown of waxy gold and white blossoms (the Arizona state flower). Silk moths and long-nosed bats sip the nectar, and the next morning orioles and butterflies take their turn, pollinating the flowers as they feed. After 24 hours the blossoms wilt, but a few weeks later scarlet fruits, resembling brilliant flowers themselves, open to offer another bounty of sweet pulp and up to a quarter-million shiny black seeds per plant.

First come the flying customers, a kaleidoscope of bright birds and butterflies and moths. Humans come too—Tohono O'odham Indians who in time-honored ritual preserve the fruit's pulp for tribal food and wine. When the fruit falls, ground-dwellers—coyotes, badgers, javelinas, coatimundis, and an occasional mule deer—begin to feast.

After all have fed, they do their part by scattering the seeds, though fewer than one in one thousand seeds may find proper conditions for germination and growth. Then in a century or so, another mighty saguaro reaches full size, a survivor like its parent, swelling its accordion-pleated trunk by as much as 16 inches to store the rare rainfall, folding its pleats in dry times to await another shower.

The desert poses little problem for its well-adapted inhabitants. About 50 kinds of cacti provide sustenance for desert-dwellers such as the desert tortoise, nibbling prickly pear fruit *(top)*, and Harris' antelope squirrel, making its way on a beavertail cactus *(above)*. A Gila monster, resting near a barrel cactus *(right)*, sneaks into birds' nests to eat eggs and young chicks.

From Sugarloaf Mountain, the breathtaking expanse of the Chiricahua Mountains seems to stretch forever. From forested foothills to canyons and upland desert, the mountains harbor an array of fascinating animals. Even a geology buff will not be disappointed. Far in the distance are renowned rock formations, born of volcanic eruptions about 25 million years ago.

The Chiricahua Mountains of southern Arizona were the last stronghold of the Apache Indians. Rising from the surrounding desert, the Chiricahuas offered watered and secluded canyons, a sanctuary against the white men who were determined to destroy the Apaches in the 1800s. Today, for the same reasons—remoteness and plenty of water—some of our rarest and most beautiful birds and other animals find a haven here.

Within a short drive from the entrance to the Chiricahuas you can ascend through five distinctive life zones, from desert through alpine. Each has its own particular flora and fauna, adapted to the temperature and moisture at that elevation. It is a dazzling experience.

The best way to approach the mountains is driving from the east through the Chihuahuan desert, where creosote bush and mesquite-dotted grasslands get so little moisture they are brown and sere most of the year. Dust devils occasionally whirl violently over exposed flats. Roadrunners pounce on lizards, and western meadowlarks perch on fenceposts along fields where Cassin's and lark sparrows dwell.

But up ahead in the blue-tinged mountains looms a sudden change. As the road enters the foothills at Portal, cottonwoods, white-patched sycamores, and Arizona cypresses appear. Acorn woodpeckers seem determined to store every acorn in the woods in their neatly rounded-out holes. Alert gray-breasted jays and bridled titmice watch where they put them. With decorative forehead tassels bobbing, Gambel's quails pick through the forest litter.

Towering cliffs flank the entrance to Cave Creek Canyon, where tall oaks arch across the noisily cascading creek alongside the road. Deep green pines and junipers stand in outline against red mountain rocks over which yellow and pale green lichens trace delicate free-form patterns. Here is the heart of birding mecca, easily accessible from the Cave Creek road which parallels the stream.

Along the rushing streams you may see birds so unusual they are not in every guidebook, like the brilliant rose-and-green eared trogon. Zone-tailed hawks often soar overhead, looking like turkey vultures except for the barred tail. If you hear a loud and very sweet trilling song, it probably came from a red-faced warbler.

"Investigate every song you hear," counsels an experienced birder. "Almost every bird you see here is one you've never seen before." Certainly a serious birder wouldn't want to miss coming here and adding the red-faced warbler and 25

TUCSON

A southwest birding hotspot, the Chiricahuas boast uncommon species that delight birdwatchers from many states and foreign countries. Thick-billed parrots *(above)*, recently reintroduced here, are the only wild parrots in this country. Elegant trogons *(above right)* migrate here from Mexico each spring. More of these colorful birds live in the Chiricahuas than anywhere else in the United States.

In the forested regions, flashes of red could be the sign of an acorn woodpecker *(below)* excavating a nesting hole. These birds also peck out rows of holes for stashing single nuts.

Arizona's Ramsey Canyon, perhaps unrivaled in the United States for its colorful variety of butterflies, shelters such delightful species as Baird's swallowtail *(below left)*.

to 40 other unusual species to his life list in just a few days. These sightings might range from a scaled quail pecking its way along a dusty roadside in the arid country to a tiny, sprightly Mexican chickadee flitting about the canopy of conifers at elevations of 8,000 feet.

Stunning birds with exotic names abound, such as the elegant (coppery-tailed) and eared trogons, sulphur-bellied flycatchers, and Hutton's vireos. Don't look for trogons where you hear the hollow *qua-qua* calls, though. These ventriloqual birds are seldom found where they seem to be. Instead, look for the flash of the trogon's raspberry breast. You also can spot three kinds of wrens, Strickland's woodpeckers, Crissal's thrashers and more. The thick-billed parrot has been reintroduced, and a flock of 16 lives in the Chiricahuas.

A fork of the Cave Creek road goes into a recreational and campground area where in the evenings elf owls chirp and whiskered screech owls call, sounding oddly like a bouncing ball on the wane. Every visitor should try to camp out at least one night. It's the best way to hear the owls and see the bats skimming over the creek water to drink and feed.

Here is where the western tanager might be seen, or the bronze cowbird. Painted redstarts nest along the stream, unmistakable in their bright patterns as they dart in and out of the understory. Remarkably, this cornucopia of birding all occurs within a few square miles.

Back on the Cave Creek road, a few miles west, the Pinery Canyon road begins, ascending steeply into open oak forest. The road switches back and forth in a steep climb. Stop on a switchback to look down over the crown of the trees below. Perhaps you'll spot the black-throated gray warbler or Grace's warbler, both of which spend May here nesting. Montezuma quail scratch for seeds along the road.

Then at Onion Saddle one road forks up to the high mountain meadows and Douglas fir woods. In spring these meadows can be carpeted with blue Rocky Mountain iris and filled with broad-tailed hummingbirds jousting over their territories. In late summer, the Chiricahuan delphiniums attract hundreds of rufous hummers.

This is probably the only place in the United States to see the Mexican chickadee. You can also look for acrobatic pygmy nuthatches, Coues' flycatchers, yellow-eyed juncos, and red-faced and olive warblers, specialties of high places.

As the road gradually begins to descend, the layers of life zones come in reverse order, slightly less dramatically because the western slopes receive less moisture. When the

Hummingbirds abound in the Chiricahuas, with 15 species recorded in Ramsey Canyon alone. Enchanted visitors might see a broad-tailed hummingbird suspended like a jewel in a paintbrush-blossom setting *(right)* or a tiny rufous hummer perched with its iridescent feathers shimmering *(above)*.

road comes out on the Sonoran desert, look along quiet stretches for one of the 75 species of mammals plus dozens of kinds of snakes, lizards, turtles, and frogs.

Almost anything that can be seen in the Chiricahua range might be seen in the Chiricahua National Monument, which also holds fantastic rock formations for which it was set aside as protected land. These formations originated in volcanic blasts that spewed molten material out of the earth 25 million years ago. It hardened into rhyolite layers, which eroded after the mountains were uplifted, leaving huge boulders and columns balanced precariously on tiny pinnacles that look as if they might collapse at any second. Instead, the strange shapes, red-gold against the sky and changing with the light, pose gorgeously for photographers.

Wildlife-watchers can enjoy the monument grounds' 18 miles of walking trails and an eight-mile scenic drive to a stunning panoramic view from Massai Point. Cliff chipmunks run along rocky ravines. Yarrow's spiny lizards, common everywhere, change from black to iridescent purple, blue, and green depending on their background.

Sit quietly at a picnic area, and a rustle in the woods may signal the approach of a dozen shy javelinas or a troup of up to 50 coatimundis digging for grubs and chirping and chattering among themselves. Wary mountain lions as well as bobcats, black bears, porcupines, and rare ocelots and jaguarundis also roam these mountains.

Monument staffers remember the day visitors kept asking about the pet lion outside. They took it as a joke; at the end of the day the staff investigated and discovered that a mountain lion—no pet—had been spending the day resting on a rock outcrop near the visitor center restrooms!

Nearby Ramsey Canyon rightly has been called the hummingbird capital of America with 15 varieties of these iridescent beauties recorded. Hummingbirds are on view almost every daylight minute at sugar-water feeders, along with western and hepatic tanagers, black-headed grosbeaks, painted redstarts, hooded orioles, and more. More butterfly species have been seen in this Nature Conservancy sanctuary than any place else in the United States. And beautiful wildflowers abound.

The catch is, Ramsey Canyon is small and must be protected from over-visitation. The six cabins usually are reserved at least a year ahead, and when the 14-car parking lot is filled, no one else is admitted. So plan and phone ahead! It's worth it to see this natural treasure.

Wary mountain lions prowl these mountains for prey such as squirrels *(below),* rabbits, and deer. A persistent visitor might be lucky enough to glimpse the elusive cat around dusk or dawn.

From roads that wind through the refuge, visitors can observe any number of animals, but sandhill cranes are definitely the stars. After daytime browsing in nearby fields, cranes return to the refuge's protective marshes.

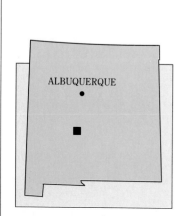

ALBUQUERQUE

NEW MEXICO

The hauntingly musical cries begin as the first light is turning the Magdalena mountains from deep blue to pink-gold, *Garooo-a-a-a! Garooo-a-a-a!* The sound can be heard for miles. It is the call of the cranes, birds which have been on earth for more than 40 million years. These are the greater sandhill cranes of Bosque del Apache National Wildlife Refuge in New Mexico, and between October and February a third of the world's population—about 15,000 birds in an average year—comes here. They are drawn by watery marshes along the upper Rio Grande, a lush wildlife oasis surrounded by arid mountains.

Soon the tall, gray, scarlet-crowned cranes are joined in their chorus by crowds of yelping white snow geese, 30,000 of them here for the winter from their nesting grounds in the Arctic, their cries blending with the gabbling of about 20,000 ducks of 14 species. The sun and their own wing clapping gradually warm the cranes as they preen and groom in the marshes where they have spent the night, often within a stone's throw of the refuge visitors' center.

In late winter the cranes that have formed pair bonds will jump up and down, their seven-foot wings spread wide. Their leaps are at one time graceful and frenetic. In adults, dancing is sometimes part of courtship. In subadults, this dancing helps to develop bonds between a pair—not unlike the maneuvering between human teenagers. At other times, the movements seem simply to be a safety valve for aggression.

Selected pairs of sandhills have served as foster parents for whooping cranes, hatching the eggs that scientists have carefully transferred from whoopers' nests elsewhere and giving a boost to the species' chances of survival.

Each morning the sandhill cranes take off, filling the air with their cries as they head out to feed. They glean harvested fields, but the refuge arranges for fields it owns to be farmed in part for the birds: a portion of the crop is left unharvested.

You can tell how cold it is on a winter morning by watching whether the cranes fly with their long, stiltlike legs trailing or tucked up in their feathers. When temperatures drop to around 29° F, the cranes tuck their legs up.

Sometimes the cranes land in fields adjoining the refuge, and coyotes, lurking behind bushes and in drainage ditches, stalk them and the snow geese. But at dusk the birds return to the safety of the marshes. As the light disappears, the numbers in the sky dwindle, and at last only one or two stragglers are left as the marsh settles down for the night.

Camouflaged by tall grasses, coyotes *(left)* sometimes stalk transient geese and cranes on the refuge. A coyote is less likely to disturb the porcupines *(right)* because an attack could cause a number of the animal's 30,000 quills to become painfully imbedded in the predator's flesh.

The last rays of an October sun are casting a rosy glow on the underside of the clouds when a soft rustling sound, like dry leaves blowing, begins. The sound is not from leaves, but from wingbeats, tens of thousands of them, as the freetail bats of Carlsbad Caverns in New Mexico come boiling out of the cave entrance.

The bats whirl upward in a counter-clockwise motion, growing louder, gaining height; then like a dark river they pour off in an undulating path toward the Pecos and Black River valleys. The tiny half-ounce creatures emerge at a rate of perhaps 5,000 a minute, some accompanied by their young.

In the valleys are ample food and water. Each bat may fly 25 to 50 miles each night and consume a third of its weight in insects. The mass of tiny, quivering bats returns to the cave just before dawn in a plunge equally dramatic to the one at dusk. In mid-August, visitors can watch the return at a "bat breakfast," complete with scrambled eggs and coffee. At the end of October, most of the bats migrate south to spend the winter in Mexico.

Seeing the bats makes some visitors shiver with a primeval feeling for this natural phenomenon that has taken place here presumably every night from May through October for at least 18,000 years. At dusk, visitors gather in an amphitheater that looks down on the cave entrance. A ranger appears just before sundown to explain how the bats live and how to watch the spectacle. Sometimes the ranger holds one of the small creatures in his hand, stretching out the delicate membrane that is its wing, to show visitors that it is not fearsome. He tells about the marvel that enables the bat to find its way and capture food in darkness by bouncing ultrasonic vibrations off anything in its path. He points out the exquisite facial structure, especially the ears, that makes echolocation possible.

"Without bats the world would be infested with insects," explains Ron Kerbo, who came as a spelunker and stayed to become an expert on bats as well. "One million bats can eat four to five tons of insects each night," he marvels. He confesses having had a bias for bats ever since he first held a bat in his hand. "I felt its wildly beating heart and knew he was not a nightmare but one like us."

The bats' cave is part of another natural marvel—the great, winding Carlsbad Caverns, filled with beautiful formations of all sizes, shapes, and colors. In the main cave some passes are accessible to wheelchairs. Other caves in the park are still being explored; visitors in good physical condition can join in cave walks by reservation.

ROSWELL

Visitors to Carlsbad Caverns
at sunset can witness the
amazing departure of tens of
thousands of freetail bats *(left
and far left)* from their cave
roost. The bats spend the night
hunting and eating, consuming
up to one-third of their weight in
moths, beetles, mosquitos, and
other flying insects. Early-rising
enthusiasts who go to the cave
at dawn are rewarded by the
thrilling sight of the bats' return.

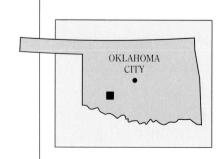

The landscape of Wichita Mountains National Wildlife Refuge seems little changed from hundreds of years ago. On the thick, vibrant prairies, longstem grasses stand up to six feet tall with roots almost as long, hoarding water and nutrients against the driest periods. Carpets of wildflowers explode in gold and blue—woodsorrel, coreopsis, prickly poppies, and prairie larkspur. Scarlet and bronze leaves cover the woods in fall. From the top of Mt. Scott, a large part of Oklahoma stretches out in all directions. Here you can stand eye to eye with a red-tailed hawk or Mississippi kite, sometimes only 20 feet away, hovering motionless in a northwest wind.

Now bison, elk, and Texas longhorns, once nearly wiped out, graze peacefully on the prairie. This is where they were brought back from the brink of extinction.

About 60 million bison, each standing up to six feet at the shoulder and weighing a ton or so, once roamed the Great

Though branded with the initials of the refuge, longhorns roam wild here and have long been a popular part of Wichita's prairie landscape. Wide-eyed visitors marvel at the steers' arching horns, which measure up to 8 feet across. In spring and summer the prairie bursts with sunflowers *(left),* coreopsis, prickly poppies, woodsorrel, and other colorful wildflowers.

Plains, seeming literally to cover the ground for miles around. But in the early 1800s, the buffalo became a target of human desire for land, profit, and amusement. Hunters killed hundreds of buffalo a day, hundreds of thousands in a year. In southern Canada's famous Red River hunt of 1850, more than 1,000 wagonloads of skins and meat were hauled away. Buffalo robes, hides, and tongues brought premium prices, and sport hunters often shot the bison and left the carcasses to rot.

By 1900 the great herds were gone and bleached bones littered the midwest prairies. The New York Zoological Park had saved some buffalo and offered to donate a nucleus herd if Congress would appropriate $15,000 to build a fence to protect the herd. In 1907 seven bulls and eight cows were put on railroad cars and shipped to Oklahoma. The great Comanche chief, Quanah Parker, came to the station with other mounted

braves to see the survivors of the plains animals that had provided meat and tepee skins for generations of their ancestors. They watched their release at the protected area in the Wichita Mountains. The buffalo again roamed the prairie, this time protected by fences and the watchful eye of government staff.

Buffalo are hardy, stolid, comeback creatures. Now young red-brown buffalo calves are born every April and the herd is kept at about 600 animals, the number this 59,000-acre wildlife refuge can maintain. Others have been moved elsewhere to start herds on other ranges.

At Wichita Mountains, wild turkeys made a similar comeback and now strut and gobble at the edge of the woods with a wonderful assortment of other creatures that came when the area gained protection. The last native elk in the Wichita Mountains was killed in 1881. A new population was

The second national wildlife refuge, Wichita was set up in 1905 mainly to protect buffalo. The current herd of 600 buffalo produces about 30 calves in April. Calves are born with soft buttonlike horns which begin to show distinctly in several months *(left)*. Gregarious prairie dogs romp in a 150-acre dog town where visitors can easily watch them. Eating grass is a favorite pastime, but a nagging itch can be more pressing *(below)*.

started here from Rocky Mountain elk and now a herd of about 500 is thriving. White-tailed deer, increasingly scarce at the end of the nineteenth century, are plentiful again.

Texas longhorns came to the New World from stock of Spanish cattle—the first shipment came with Columbus—but some escaped and became wild. When the Civil War ended, an estimated six million ranged over the southwest. From 1860 to 1890 Texas cowboys drove about 10 million of them north on the Chisholm Trail. But longhorns, which weigh up to a ton and have horns up to eight feet tip-to-tip, can be hard beasts to handle and are less meaty than domestic varieties. So with the closing of the open range, the longhorn, too, disappeared. A nationwide search turned up 30 true longhorns that in 1927 were brought from Texas and Mexico to Wichita Mountains, where the herd has thrived.

Mountain lions are here now, though not often seen. Coyotes are fairly common, though wary, and bobcats and gray foxes have been sighted.

The refuge boundaries are still fenced to keep bison from wandering onto surrounding farms, and parts of the refuge are fenced to protect against over-visitation during sensitive times, such as when longhorns are calving. But whenever practical, the animals roam free, and visitors can often observe them close at hand.

Bison sometimes graze around campgrounds and picnic tables. Campers almost certainly will hear coyotes and great horned owls at night, and unless they put food away securely, they probably will meet a raccoon face-to-face.

Prairie dogs traditionally have shared the prairie scene at Wichita Mountains, with delighted visitors watching their exuberant, frolicsome family life in a 150-acre prairie dog "town." The Wichita Mountains colony has been inundated by floods several times, but the refuge staff is planning to move the prairie dogs to more protected spots.

Throughout the year visitors can go on field trips that include eagle-watching (both bald and golden) and wildlife-watching under the stars. Elk "bugling" tours are held in the fall when males, whose antler racks may measure three feet across, go looking for females. A refuge staffer blows into an elk-bugler, a turkey call attached to a long hose that gives it the vibrancy of a bull elk's windpipe. What comes out is something between a whistle, a grunt, and a bellow. What answers is a male elk, wild-eyed, hair standing on end—and chagrined not to find another elk. Sometimes other elk answer until the calls echo musically around the granite canyons. At the end of

the rutting season the bulls are exhausted and hoarse, the winners in this mating game so debilitated that they are frequently displaced by challengers the next time around.

In all seasons except winter, Mississippi kites are often seen. Common all year are great blue herons, bobwhite quail, Carolina chickadees, Bewick's wrens and rufous-crowned sparrows. A small, remote colony of endangered black-capped vireos lives here as well.

A scenic drive crosses the refuge and visitors can enjoy two campgrounds and miles of hiking trails, some of them in areas with no roads or other traces of human existence. Visitors who spend time in the wilderness come to know Wichita Mountains as they could in no other way. Refuge staffers say it can work the other way around, too: visitors get to know themselves better, and Wichita Mountains helped.

Each year in late October a pair of great white birds settles gracefully over the Texas Gulf marsh calling *Ker-loo! Ker-lee-oo!* in bell-like notes that can be heard for three miles or more. As the birds land, there is no mistaking them: their black-tipped wings stretch up to seven feet from end to end; standing five feet tall, they tower over the herons and egrets already there.

The first whooping cranes of the season—the birds that made "endangered species" a household term—are back in winter residence at Aransas National Wildlife Refuge, their perilous migration from Canada's Northwest Territories behind them. The rest of the cranes will arrive over the next few weeks, usually in pairs, each pair often accompanied by a single, rusty-speckled youngster. Gradually they stake out feeding territories, each family claiming about 400 acres of marsh around the edges of the peninsula that juts like a thumb into the Gulf of Mexico.

The refuge was established in 1937 to protect waterfowl, but in the years since, the words "Aransas" and "whooping crane" have become intertwined in the minds of nature lovers. Whooping cranes have become the focus at Aransas, and saving them its hope. Each arrival is carefully noted. The count here in 1988 was 138. Including others in captivity and in a foster-parent flock at Bosque del Apache National Wildlife Refuge in New Mexico *(see page 76),* the total of whooping cranes in existence nears 200. A visitor to Aransas can be virtually certain to catch a glimpse of them between early November and April first.

It was not always so.

The comeback—and one must always say "thus far," barring an oil spill or other such calamity—has been dramatic. No other bird has captured world attention as the whooping crane has, and understandably so.

Partly it is their regal beauty. The cranes are tall, almost all white with striking crimson face patches. Their graceful courtship dances are legendary. A pair will face each other with outstretched necks and bobbing heads, prancing from foot to foot and bowing deeply with wings open as if to embrace the partner. Sometimes they toss grass and sticks into the air and leap as high as 12 feet. It all ends when the female bows low and the male mounts her. Sometimes in a glorious finale both of them will throw their heads back and call together for several minutes in what seems to be an expression of irrepressible joy. It is an awesome performance that North American Indians mimicked in ceremonial dances.

Famed for its wintering whooping cranes, Aransas is the last stop on the cranes' migratory journey from nesting grounds in Canada. Whether wading in Gulf waters *(left),* preening *(right),* or performing courtship dances, the whoopers' five-foot stature and bright scarlet foreheads make them unforgettable sights.

Next page: While not nearly so unusual as the whooping cranes, white-tailed deer have their own elegance and beauty, which is enhanced by a backdrop of the refuge's magnificent live oaks.

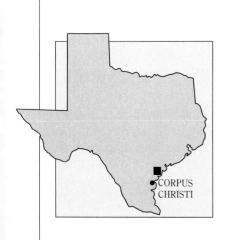

CORPUS
CHRISTI

Reddish egrets *(below),* an endangered species in Texas, find shelter in Aransas' freshwater ponds and sloughs. A number of other endangered species—whoopers, brown pelicans, and peregrine falcons—also take refuge here.

Part of the cranes' appeal is their piercing call. It is eerie and unforgettable and epitomizes the whooper's wild nature. "When we hear his call we hear no mere bird. . . . He is the symbol of our untamable past," naturalist Aldo Leopold said. The call is thought to re-cement psychological bonds between the paired birds, which mate for life. It issues from a remarkable windpipe that does not go straight down the neck as in other birds but coils around for a length of up to five feet, about half of which is inside the breastbone. A human with such a windpipe would suffocate, our respiratory system being much less efficient than a bird's. In the whooper, the long windpipe and intricate network of air passages make possible a resonance like a French horn's.

All this can be seen and heard by almost any winter visitor touring Aransas on boats that leave nearby Rockport each day. The cranes are used to the boats, and visitors almost always get a fine view of one of the world's rarest creatures. To get a close-up photo, take a telephoto lens and pick a boat trip going out at low tide, when the birds wander far out on the mud flats near the channel. Because other beautiful wading birds also are out on the flats—great blue herons and American egrets, for example—the boat trip is a thrilling experience. You also can get a good view of the wildlife from an observation tower on the refuge where telescopes cover much of the marsh.

Admiration for the cranes grows when you consider the hazardous 5,000-mile round trip they undertake every year between Aransas and their nesting grounds in the bullrush bogs of Canada's Wood Buffalo National Park. Their long wings form a perfect airfoil and enable flight at speeds of about

With their armorlike shells and ambling walk, armadillos are unmistakable trademarks of south Texas' open spaces. To ward off attacks from predators, some armadillo species roll into a virtually impenetrable ball.

30 miles an hour. Usually the trip takes between two and six weeks. It is fraught with danger not only from natural hazards, such as storms, but also from power lines and from hunters who shoot first and look later.

Once whooping cranes ranged over most of the interior United States, but their wilderness lifestyle could not accommodate human intrusion. Little by little their population was whittled away as they were shot for food or trophies and their marshy solitudes were drained and planted with crops. In 1941 only 22 whooping cranes were known to exist in the world. Most of these arrived each winter at Aransas, but when they left in the spring to nest and hatch their chicks, no one knew where they went.

Then in 1954 a helicopter pilot returning from a forest fire in Wood Buffalo National Park radioed the Canadian Wildlife Service that he had spotted two adult whooping cranes and one fledgling. Scientists tracked down the secluded nesting site. Since then the Canadian and American governments have cooperated to protect the cranes and the birds' numbers have gradually increased, though they still face hazards.

While whooping cranes have made Aransas one of our best known refuges, its fame would be justified in any case by the huge numbers of other creatures that have found homes there. The bird list is one of the longest of any refuge—373 species at last count. Cormorants move along offshore in rafts of 1,000 or more, so closely packed that they make an enormous black mass in the water. All nine American members of the rail family have been seen at Jones Lake and other sites, along with least and pied-billed grebes, least bitterns, and any of 15 kinds of beautiful wading birds. From mid-April to early May, warblers in breeding plumage—magnolia, yellow, chestnut-sided, baybreasted and many others—may concentrate in great numbers. A dozen species can sometimes be seen in a single tree.

It is not unusual to see three imperiled species simultaneously from the observation tower: the whoopers plus brown pelicans and reddish egrets. The count goes up if a peregrine falcon whizzes by or a piping plover or wood stork strolls out on the flats.

In one pass around the 16-mile auto-tour loop road, you may see dozens of white-tailed deer with fine racks of antlers. Or you may spy spotted fawns peeking out in the spring. The loop road winds through such varied habitats (woods, meadows, freshwater ponds, salt marshes, and tidal flats) that any of the thousands of plants and animals may be seen from cars.

In autumn, it is not unusual to see six or more different raptors (northern harriers, merlins, kestrels, and Cooper's, red-shouldered, and red-tailed hawks) peering from the tops of trees or old snags. Meanwhile several flycatchers forage from shrubs at a lower level. Two dozen pearly peach and gray scissortailed flycatchers may appear during fall migration, hovering or diving on insects, their long tail feathers streaming like banners behind them. Businesslike loggerhead shrikes wait for small frogs or lizards, sometimes impaling a kill on a nearby thorn for safekeeping. "My favorite bird," says refuge manager Brent Giezentanner, ". . . the body of a sparrow with the heart of an eagle!"

Tremendous spreading live oaks provide a bounty of acorns which attract shy, nearsighted javelinas. The picnic area is a good place to watch for these, especially on overcast days. You can tell javelinas from feral hogs by the tail. If it's tucked up against the body, it's a javelina. When two javelinas are standing side by side and rubbing vigorously, they are exchanging scent signals, important in social relationships.

About 250 alligators live here around fresh water, including one 13-footer that haunts Thomas Slough.

Wildflowers are glorious. The visitor center lawn and roadsides can be solid gold with primroses and, later, Indian blanket. Christmas berry and brilliant purple beautyberry bushes are their breathtaking counterpart in October.

While the marshy refuge is best known for saving the cranes, its protected character has created a haven for many other creatures as well. The worldwide excitement generated a half century ago by the cranes' battle for survival also spilled over into support for development of other refuges to save and harbor other species. In this way, the cranes, which showed that they could make it with a little help from us, have helped save many others, including alligators and brown pelicans, eagles and peregrine falcons.

anta Ana has been called the jewel of the national wildlife refuge system, and its jewel-like inhabitants greet
visitors almost as soon as they enter. Orange and
black Altamira orioles whistle from the ebony trees.
Green jays scream with beaks full of berries, and buff-bellied
hummingbirds flit in and among the lilies called scarlet Turk's-
cap. Mexican chachalacas, appearing half-pheasant, half-
turkey, warn "cut-it-out" as they emerge from behind a cur-
tain of curly gray Spanish moss. And scores of other colorful
birds, many rarely seen elsewhere, are common at this
2,080-acre tract of dense tropical vegetation along the lower
Rio Grande, a muddy brown river on the border with Mexico.

Part of Santa Ana's appeal is how compressed it all is.
Most of the great refuges are large, sprawling over hundreds
of thousands of acres. But Santa Ana is at once so tiny and so
vibrant with colorful birds, butterflies, and plants that the
word "jewel" comes inevitably to mind.

Verdant tropical habitat like Santa Ana's used to spread
all along the Rio Grande, offering mud flats for shorebirds and
streamside terraces, bottomland woods, and upland thorn
forests as nesting and feeding places for a vast array of creatures. But since 1900, much of the valley has been cleared for
crops. Santa Ana remains as an island haven for birds as well
as four-footed wildlife. Ocelots and jaguarundis are too wary
to be seen often, but a half-dozen reports a year attest to their
existence here. Javelinas root around in the sandy forest floor
and mountain lions are even spotted now and then.

Visitors come from all over the United States to marvel
at the dozens of colorful and remarkable bird species: the olive
sparrow, long-billed thrasher, Couch's kingbird, Inca dove,
painted bunting, great kiskadee, brown-crested flycatcher,
black-bellied whistling duck, least grebe, crested caracara,
and northern jacana, to name a few. Nowhere else in the
United States is so much birding excitement crowded into
such a small space. On a cool winter morning a New York birdwatcher who has flown down for the day to see a once-in-a-
lifetime rarity may be chatting under his breath with a visitor
from West Germany, both of them with binoculars glued to
their eyes. The Santa Ana bird list contains an astonishing 380
species, longest of any United States refuge—yet in just a few
square miles! Of these, 31 are found nowhere else in the
country outside the Rio Grande Valley.

As many as 35,000 migrating broadwinged hawks have
been counted in a day, along with hundreds of wood-
warblers—Blackburnian, orange-crowned, chestnut-sided,

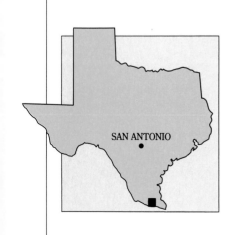

SAN ANTONIO

Situated on the river boundary between the United States and Mexico, Santa Ana refuge offers the chance to see some plants and animals typical of both countries. Mexico's national symbol, the crested caracara *(far left),* appears frequently in south Texas. When the bird feels threatened, its bright orange face blanches and its long crest feathers flare upward. Along the river, a blooming yucca provides a massive perch for a meadowlark *(left).*

Christmas bird count, an annual ritual when birders all over the country go out to take a census, hoping always for the sight of a rarity to spice the listing. Birders quickly came from all over the United States and several foreign countries to see the crane hawk devouring frogs by Pintail Lake.

Santa Ana has become a refuge, too, for many uncommon plants. More than 450 kinds of trees, shrubs, wildflowers and fruiting vines have been catalogued, including two national champion trees (the Brasil and guayacan) and some leafy species so specialized in their requirements that their entire range is limited to a few acres. Depending on the rainfall, wildflowers can start blooming in mid-February and keep it up until late November, attracting dozens of butterfly species, many found nowhere else in the country.

The seven-mile auto-tour route winds through the refuge and three walking trails branch off it, one with wheelchair access and a rail for the sight-impaired. During crowded winter periods the tour road is closed to cars, and visitors instead take an open tram with naturalist guides. Stops are made so visitors can get off to hike or photograph. Photoblinds are available with feeders located so photographers can virtually count on the appearance of chachalacas, green jays, and white-tipped doves, sometimes several dozen at one time!

Equally fascinating if less well known is Bentsen State Park, another island of lower Rio Grande habitat located between two resacas, lakelike sections of a river that have been cut off by a new channel. Anything that appears at Santa Ana may also be seen at Bentsen. Bentsen supports such unusual species as the tiny beardless flycatcher, clay-colored robin, and the rare hook-billed kite (watch for these soaring over the hiking trail entrance in the morning). Abundant white snails make good fare for roadrunners, which open them by beating them on rocks. Mesquite trees that grow six feet tall elsewhere are 40-foot giants here. Some of the best nature-watching is around the park's secluded campsites, and even stealthy bobcats are sometimes sighted.

The Interior department has proposed setting aside and linking strategic wildlife areas, including Santa Ana and Bentsen, along 200 miles of the lower Rio Grande. The corridor would be a combination of federal, state, and private lands. Such a corridor could provide sanctuary not only for the colorful birds found in Santa Ana and Bentsen, but for animals like the ocelot, which cannot easily move between isolated chunks of habitat but which might begin to thrive if it could roam in a wider, protected setting.

yellow-throated, black-throated green, and a dozen other species. Huge flights of white-winged doves have roosted here, seeming to fill every tree.

Migrating birds come partly because of the strategic location. Santa Ana is at the convergence of two major flyways, the Mississippi and the central, so that great flocks of migrants funnel through in both spring and fall. Some stay to winter. It is also within the northernmost range of many Mexican and South American species, so that birds of two hemispheres mingle here in one locale.

Three kinds of kingfishers dive for their dinner in Willow Lake: ringed, green, and belted. At least 73 species of birds nest, including Harris' hawks, black-shouldered and hook-billed kites, groove-billed ani, white-winged doves, and pauraques, whose red eyes glow when reflecting the late afternoon Texas sun.

And the list grows constantly. Recently a crane hawk showed up for the first appearance ever recorded in this country. Happily, the bird's appearance coincided with the

The flashing of its multicolor feathers sometimes gives away the shy painted bunting *(left)*. First-time observers may think they are seeing some exotic pet bird which has escaped from its cage. Another in Santa Ana's parade of colorful wildlife is the green hairstreak butterfly, which sips nectar from primrose *(far left)* and other blossoms.

THE ROCKY MOUNTAINS

A mountain goat and a photographer *(below)* give each other a cautious once-over in an amiable confrontation at Glacier.

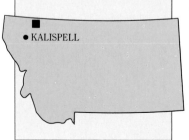

Preceding page: Carved by mighty glaciers, this rugged part of Montana teems with wildlife. White-blossomed wildflowers *(right)* were named beargrass by Lewis and Clark because the explorers often noticed bears moving among them. Bears do not eat the plants, except for the succulent leaf base in spring.

● KALISPELL

Glacier National Park is a wild place, a million-acre hunk of northern Montana that is one of the biggest, rawest, most beautiful wild places left in America.
The northern Rockies ripple and bulge along the length of Glacier. Life-giving water shimmers and splashes throughout the park in the form of hundreds of lakes, nearly a thousand miles of rivers and creeks, and countless waterfalls. During the summer the valleys burst with beargrass and other wildflowers. About 50 glaciers, remnants of the ice-age behemoths that carved out those valleys, still cling to high mountain cirques. Above the tree line spreads the ethereal alpine tundra, and at lower elevations the forest is thick with nearly impenetrable stands of lodgepole pine and vaulted communities of western white pine, Douglas fir, and gigantic western red cedar. Even the name of the road that labors across the rugged park, Going-to-the-Sun Road, bespeaks Glacier's wildness.

This robust and unspoiled land seems so distant from civilization that it's easy to imagine Glacier's dense forests as they were hundreds of years ago, teeming with wildlife. One can imagine that wolverines, wolves, mountain lions, and grizzlies—animals that westward expansion virtually wiped out—still stalk prey in Glacier's dark forests.

Well, as a matter of fact, they do.

Wolves, which need many square miles in which to roam, are a sure sign of Glacier's wild expanses. While visitors are unlikely to see wolves, they might be lucky enough to hear them, sometimes in bone-chilling choruses. Protected by dense fur and able to trot for miles to seek food, the wolves find little to fear from long, harsh winters near the Canadian border.

The strongest indicator of Glacier's wildness is the presence of gray wolves. Wolves establish immense territories, so they need wilderness and lots of it. They also need an ample supply of their favorite prey (Glacier has elk, deer, and moose), and, if history is any indication, wolves need to stay clear of humans. Between 1883 and 1918 more than 80,000 wolves were shot, trapped, or poisoned in Montana alone.

Gray wolves hadn't bred in the western United States for 50 years, and in the early 1980s, scientists talked about reintroducing wolves to Glacier's wide expanses. But in 1985 a pack of 12 wolves simply trotted from Canada into Glacier, making the scientists' discussions moot. The next spring one of the pack's females bore a litter of pups. By 1987 four packs were known to be in or near Glacier. (The wolves move freely back and forth from Glacier to Canada.) Kate Kendall, a research biologist at Glacier, was skiing in the North Fork area when a pack began howling nearby. "Hearing those wolves made me feel like I was really in the wilderness," she says.

Kendall was lucky, and she spends a lot of time tramping around in Glacier. The odds of a casual visitor seeing or even hearing *Canis lupus* are slim. But those who beat the odds will glimpse a remarkable animal that can run for miles through deep snow, sleep cozily in the open when it's 40 degrees below, and bite into a moose's snout and hang on as the moose flings the wolf about like a dog shaking a rag.

Most remarkable, perhaps, is the wolves' social nature. Both pups and adults play vigorously, chasing birds and leaping out at each other from hiding places to inflict a good scare. They speak volumes with subtle facial expressions that rival a raised eyebrow from Laurence Olivier. Wolves' most famous social behavior is howling, which apparently is used to assemble the pack, to locate one another, to assert ownership over their territory, and to avoid tangling with other packs. Instead of howling on the same note, wolves harmonize, which can make five wolves sound like 50.

The only animal in North America that has been as feared, revered, and misunderstood as the wolf is the grizzly bear, and it, too, has found safe harbor in Glacier. About 200 of these hulking omnivores range across the park. Though grizzly bears aren't the homicidal monsters of B-grade horror movies, neither are they cuddly, oversized teddy bears. An aroused grizzly can cover 50 yards in three seconds. At the wrong time in the wrong place a grizzly bear is always the wrong animal to meet.

For safety's sake, the park service lists tips for avoiding

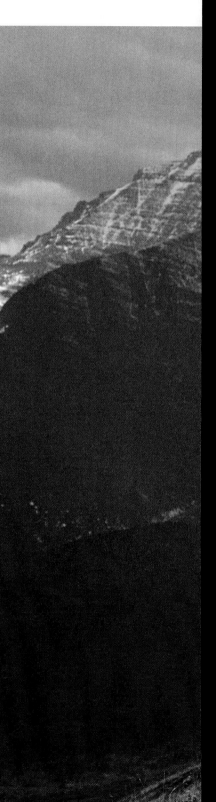

Steep pinnacles make an improbable resting place, except for mountain goats *(left)*. They climb there with aplomb, thanks to hooves that guarantee good traction. Bighorn rams *(below)* pass the day chewing their cuds.

close encounters of the furred kind, and visitors are urged to take the recommendations seriously. As Kathy Dimont of Glacier's research department says, "Some people don't believe all the precautions are necessary. They think they can't die when they're on vacation."

Hikers will come across grizzlies now and then, and if the bears are far enough away—a quarter of a mile is nice—it's safe to sit quietly and watch them. In the early summer someone tromping through the high country may see grizzlies digging for glacier lily bulbs, a prized delicacy. Kate Kendall, who has studied bears for years, says that it takes immense strength to unearth the lily's hazelnut-size bulbs: "Bears make it look easy, but I've tried to dig them up myself in the rocky, hard soil and it's really tough, even with a knife. Sometimes the grizzlies will dig their front claws into a huge piece of sod and then jerk back with their whole bodies and rip out a chunk of sod six inches deep and a couple of feet square. And they'll do it for hours on end."

Kendall says that people sometimes spot grizzlies from the road, the safest place from which to watch them. She cites some shaded areas along Going-to-the-Sun Road where snow slides last into the summer. Grizzlies have used one of these snowy chutes as transportation, sliding down it for maybe 100 yards with a few starts and stops. Kendall recalls seeing two cubs tumbling around on the snow while their mother grazed nearby. At one point they slid about 20 feet down a slope and, thinking that was great fun, climbed back up and scooted down a couple more times.

Any place wild enough for wolves and grizzlies is bound to harbor virtually all the other species that belong in the ecosystem, and Glacier is just such a place. A short hike along a forest stream or lake might turn up a moose, a river otter, or a mink, and almost certainly will pass by a beaver lodge and a muskrat nest and maybe one of the occupants. Up in the high country hoary marmots and pikas scramble among the rock piles and bighorn sheep scramble over them. Ospreys and great horned owls beat the air overhead with their powerful wings; loons and harlequin ducks grace the park's waterways with their luminous colors and natty markings.

Occasionally the congregations of animals will astonish even the most experienced wildlife watcher. Photographer Bill McRae recalls pulling off Going-to-the-Sun Road near Avalanche Creek one time and finding a veritable ark-full of animals gathered in front of him. "I could see a black bear in an avalanche chute on the east side, some white-tailed deer not

30 feet away, five bull elk on the east side of the road, a grizzly and some mountain goats above the grizzly, two mule deer only a couple of hundred feet from the grizzly, and a moose along a creek. And to top it all off, I spotted a ruffed grouse nearby drumming on a log."

Of all the animals in Glacier, the mountain goat may be the favorite, winning visitors' hearts with their oddly proportioned bodies, their lugubriously long faces, and those droopy white beards. They're also frequently seen, which boosts their popularity.

But when they shift into high gear, mountain goats no longer look goofy. They are climbers par excellence, negotiating a rocky mountain the way a squirrel takes on a tree. Mountain goats are born to climb—kids begin challenging boulders within a few hours after birth—and they spend much of their lives on slopes of 40 degrees or more. Obviously their bodies have adapted to the rigors of climbing. Look at the size of their husky chests and massive shoulder humps relative to their slender hindquarters. That allows the goats to haul themselves up steep inclines with their front feet. Mountain goats can hook one front hoof on a ledge above them and drag themselves up, essentially doing a one-handed pull-up.

One evening while hiking on the Garden Wall, Bill McRae saw several mountain goats feeding in a meadow set high on the wall. As he watched, a grizzly came into sight about a quarter of a mile away and the goats took off—right up the wall. Now, the Garden Wall is a glacial arête, a ridge honed to a fine edge eons ago when glaciers squeezed along on both sides of it. It's so steep that people going up it must often haul themselves up hand-over-hand. Yet these spooked goats *ran* up the last 1,000 feet of the wall, the most precipitous part, and disappeared over the top.

Watching mountain goats may momentarily suppress thoughts of furtive wolves and dangerous grizzlies, but the presence of such animals in Glacier can never be completely forgotten, particularly during a hike in the remote stretches of the backcountry.

Such predators make the ecosystem more complete, and offer a fuller experience to those who want to see wildlife in the most natural context available. And the remote but real threat that a grizzly might drag us humans into the food chain makes us—if even just for an afternoon's hike—a part of the system. It's a little frightening, yet that tiny measure of participation draws us into an intimacy with Glacier that is rare and wonderful.

Grizzlies are quick, powerful, and unpredictable, so rangers advise hikers to wear "bear bells." The jingling noise may warn a grizzly that someone's coming and reduce the odds of a dangerous encounter. Even from a distance, a wind-fluffed grizzly is still a striking sight.

Visitors to the beautiful Teton mountains *(right)* alternate between gazing at the striking peaks and marvelling at the abundance of wildlife. The sharp-toothed granite mountains were created from some of the oldest rock in North America.

If handed some crayons and asked to draw mountains, a child might produce a picture that resembles the Teton Range—sharp and high, rising suddenly without the distraction of foothills. The tallest, Grand Teton, cuts through thin air to 13,770 feet. Yet, as the name of their highest peak reflects, the Tetons are more than pretty, more than tall—they are grand, and their grandeur tends to overshadow the other attributes of Wyoming's Grand Teton National Park. Mountain-mesmerized visitors may sometimes overlook a moose feeding nearby or an eagle gliding overhead, and that's a shame because the park brims with these and other animals.

Most of the animals live in Jackson Hole, the valley that constitutes the eastern half of the park. Pronghorns and bison graze the sagebrush country. Moose forage in beaver ponds, clear water cascading from the bulls' antlers when they raise their heads to eat the aquatic plants they've chewed off. Great blue herons stilt along near the banks of one of the braids of the Snake River while bald eagles patrol the shallows. Coyotes range everywhere in the valley, keeping an eye out for prey. Of course, just as the mountains don't have a monopoly on beauty, the valley doesn't have a monopoly on wildlife. Bighorn sheep, porcupines, lynx, marmots, black bears, pikas, and martens spend some of their time at higher elevations.

For overall wildlife viewing in Grand Teton there's no better approach for a visitor than to prowl near water. For example, you'd likely sight at least one of the 15 pairs of rare trumpeter swans. Research biologist Pete Hayden says some of the swans nest in plain view on larger ponds, though people should use binoculars and avoid approaching closely enough to disturb them. "You can see the little birds come off the nest. You even can see the eggs," says Hayden.

Trumpeter swans defend their nesting territories passionately. Hayden remembers when a nesting pair driven from their home tried to move in on the pond of an established couple. The Teton swans flew madly at the intruders, trumpeting as only a trumpeter swan can, and sent them packing. The intruders tried again, mounting a fresh invasion as often as every 20 minutes, and the established swans assaulted them every time, skimming over the water as if to run them over, until the interlopers finally went elsewhere.

About 30 pairs of ospreys also nest in Grand Teton. These intricately marked hawks are wonderful fishers and often can be seen flying with slow deliberation over lakes, streams, and rivers. When an osprey spies a likely looking meal, it stops abruptly and hovers, beating its wings rapidly.

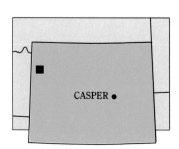

CASPER ●

A stately trumpeter swan *(left)* can turn fierce in a hurry if anything threatens its nest, fighting off intruders with outstretched wings and deep, booming calls. The largest waterfowl in North America, trumpeters can be seen all year here and in Yellowstone. Near extinction in the 1930s, they made a comeback after being given protection.

Anything that bothers a moose calf will quickly be in trouble with its fast-moving mother, whose powerful forefeet and jaws make formidable weapons. Cows with calves *(below)* stay alert, even when eating. The Tetons' green sanctuary *(left)* also shelters hundreds of bison, deer, and smaller mammals.

When the moment is right, the osprey will fold its wings and cannonball into the water talons first, raising a splash and sometimes going completely under. About one out of three times, an osprey will emerge clutching a wriggling fish.

At some point while waiting patiently, a wildlife watcher might think he sees one of the Tetons shouldering through the willows; that'd be a moose. Bull moose weigh up to 1,800 pounds and stand up to seven-and-a-half feet at the shoulder, nearly as high as an average ceiling. Throw in the head and antlers and you're talking cathedral ceiling.

Imposing as moose are, it's difficult not to regard them as a bit comical: something about that lobe of useless hair and skin that dangles from a moose's throat, those satellite-dish antlers, and the preposterous snout. However, don't think of moose as characters from a Dr. Seuss book unless you want to risk having the oobleck kicked out of you. Cows protect their calves and will charge anything, humans included, to defend them. And bulls during their rut will charge anything alive and even some things that aren't, such as boulders and fences.

Hundreds of elk also roam Grand Teton, but elk are more difficult to spot during the warm weather because they spend most of the day in tall timber. Elk aren't commonly seen until mid-September, when they start toward their winter range, sometimes in groups of 200 or 300. If they aren't seen they'll surely be heard; bulls gripped by reproductive tension make the land resound with their bugling, one of the most unusual sounds in the animal kingdom. Imagine a jazz clarinetist improvising on a theme of screeching car brakes, and you'll get a flavor of what bugling during the rut sounds like.

When the cool of fall slides into the cold of winter, nearly all of the park's elk migrate to the National Elk Refuge, a chunk of land that abuts the southern end of Grand Teton. This usually takes place in November, and it can happen abruptly if nasty weather is in the air. Jim Griffin, assistant refuge manager, saw about 2,000 elk enter the refuge en masse early one morning. "It was spectacular," he recalls. "There was a strand of elk strung out for at least two miles. They were coming two to twelve abreast: bulls, cows, calves, and spikes. Not hurrying, just walking slowly. It was a quiet morning and I could hear bugling, squealing, a lot of chattering, and a kind of soft hoofbeat noise, like quiet thunder."

What Griffin witnessed was a dramatic moment in the annual Greater Yellowstone elk migration, one of the last great large-mammal migrations in America. The 7,000 to 9,000 elk that move from Grand Teton and other public lands to the elk refuge each winter constitute a significant portion of that seasonal tide. Encountering multitudes of these elk on the move, as Griffin did, is largely a matter of luck, but seeing them once they've settled in on the refuge is a sure thing. Partly to prevent people from walking or skiing out to the elk herds, which would disturb these sensitive animals, the refuge takes visitors out in horse-drawn sleighs to view the elk. The elk are accustomed to these visits, so the sleighs approach to within just a few yards. On a cold day, say around zero, the elk may just be quietly grazing or chewing their cud, or even eerily silent. "People see the elk being so placid," says Griffin, "and they ask, 'are these really wild animals?' But the basic winter mode for elk is to conserve energy."

When the mercury fights its way up to 20 or 30 degrees and it's sunny, the elk become more active. Cows and their calves squeal to communicate, producing chatter called "elk talk." Younger bulls spar a lot, snorting clouds of vapor into the chilled air and clacking antlers with each other. The scene evokes the halcyon days of American wildlife: thousands of elk darkening the snowy flats, thick-furred coyotes lurking at the edges of the herd, and, above all, the spires of the Tetons filling the sky, imbuing the tableau with an aura of eternity.

F ish watching? No, that's not the premise of a Monty Python skit but a bona fide activity at Yellowstone National Park. Granted, trout may not set the hearts of wildlife watchers aflutter quite as much as mountain lions or bison do, but the fact that Yellowstone offers even something as arcane as fish watching makes a point; the variety of wildlife that can be viewed within the park is astonishing.

The numbers aren't bad, either: 2,700 bison, 300 black bears, 30,000 elk, 250 bighorn sheep, 2,000 mule deer, 500 pronghorn—and that's just some of the large mammals. River otters, porcupines, trumpeter swans, Canada geese, marmots, bald eagles, and many other birds and smaller mammals also bolster Yellowstone's status as the best display of large mammals in the lower 48 states. People who feared that the extensive fires of 1988 had decimated Yellowstone's wildlife needn't worry. The fires ultimately benefitted wildlife by creating clearings and stimulating growth of grasses and forbs.

Unfortunately, another large mammal proliferates in the northwest corner of Wyoming during the summer, overpopulating its range, and that's *Homo sapiens*. Millions of fair-weather visitors tax Yellowstone's facilities and crowd its roads, sometimes creating Los Angeles-like traffic jams that are the antithesis of the wilderness experience. Too often a bison or elk will wander into view only to be surrounded by a camera-wielding mob. An easy way to avoid the crowds is to head into the backcountry, but there's an even better alternative: go to Yellowstone when the mercury slides to 20 degrees and three feet of snow covers the ground.

Sure, winter makes visiting a little tougher, but that's

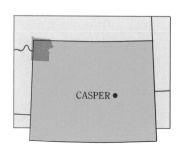

CASPER ●

The world's oldest national park shelters trumpeter swans on Yellowstone River *(left)* and hundreds of elk in its forests. In summer, elk sport antlers covered with velvet *(below),* but by late August, the velvet, which supplies nutrients for antler growth, hangs in shreds. As winter nears, Yellowstone also changes character. Minus the summer traffic and heat, it offers another bonus: wildlife is still abundant and easy to see.

why on an average winter day only about a thousand people visit the 2.2-million-acre park. That is 2,200 acres per person, enough wildness and solitude for most anyone. For those who don't want unmitigated solitude, the park service and the park concessioners provide various activities and amenities during the winter, including two lodges, snowcoach tours, guided cross-country ski trips, warming huts, ranger-led snowmobile excursions, and snowshoe hikes.

During the winter, the animals gather in relatively small, accessible areas instead of fanning out all over the park as they do during the summer. Says Frank Balthis, a photographer who worked as a ranger-naturalist in the park for four years, "It's hard to go out and not see animals. Yellowstone is one of the best places for winter wildlife viewing." The snow and cold drive most of the herbivores to lower elevations and to thermal areas, where foraging for vegetation is much easier in the shallower snow. And, of course, predators follow their prey.

Arguably, the finest winter wildlife watching occurs around Mammoth Hot Springs and along the 47-mile road between Mammoth and the northeast entrance. Elk, mule deer, and bison tramp all over the Mammoth area, not going much out of their way to avoid humans. During a stay at the Mammoth lodge one winter I sometimes had to skirt elk and bison as I strolled to breakfast at the nearby restaurant.

In a four-hour drive along the road from Mammoth one winter morning, I saw more wildlife than I'd expect to see in a week during the summer. Elk and bison cropped up, sometimes in substantial herds and often close to the road. Many times I got to watch them feeding. The bison, their massive shoulder humps thick with muscle, are superbly adapted to grazing in the snow. With a few powerful swipes of their heads they shovel away many cubic feet of snow and uncover edible vegetation. With only their spindly legs as tools, elk have a more difficult time scratching out a meal.

I also saw some animals from the road that I hadn't seen back in Mammoth, including a handsome sea duck called a Barrow's goldeneye, two coyotes feeding on elk carcasses, and many bighorn sheep. On one hill six mature bighorn rams grazed, so close that I almost could count the growth rings on their curled horns. The rams looked beautiful, both in their own right and as the foreground of a masterpiece set against the hillside, the surrounding dark green forest, the mountains that rose above the forest, and a sky the incongruous color of a tropical lagoon.

Most likely I was able to watch those rams from only

Many animals here have grown used to visitors, so if humans stay on the trails *(left)* they can view wildlife like this cow elk with no trouble, often in a spellbinding setting of steam and snow. Wearing its winter camouflage, an agile ermine *(above)* prowls Yellowstone's woodlands. Come spring, it will molt to a chocolate brown coat.

about 100 feet away because I stayed on the road. Yellowstone's wild animals have developed a sense of where people belong, so that by sticking to a road, a trail, or one of the boardwalks that crisscross the thermal areas, it's possible to pass close by such animals without disturbing them. Once, while skiing a trail near Old Faithful, I noticed that a huge, seven-point bull elk was nonchalantly reclining in the trees fewer than five yards from me. I stared for at least a minute and he never budged. Still, whatever the situation, never crowd an animal, especially one that is acting skittish.

Close behind Mammoth and Lamar Valley in the wildlife standings are Yellowstone's thermal areas, where the warmth keeps snow depths tolerable or even melts snow away. Where thermal run-off pours into rivers, trumpeter swans, Canada geese, and ducks can be spotted in their version of a swimming pool. However, most animals that stick it out in the

depths of the park in winter gather around the geyser basins.

In these frigid months, the Old Faithful area looks ghostly but beautiful. Steam hisses from slits in the ground and drifts across the land like mist on an English moor. Mud pits boil and bubble, geyser cones pock the landscape like miniature volcanoes, and sulphurous fumes float on the wind. When temperatures drop far below zero, steam condenses on trees and shrouds them in ice, creating the famous "ghost trees." Watching animals moving through this raw world is downright eerie: picture a snow-covered bison silently appearing in the blowing steam like a ship slipping through a thick fog.

People who have spent time at Old Faithful in winter report many strange sights. One observer watched a grizzly trying to scoop up a boiled bison that had fallen into a hot spring, but the hungry bear kept burning its paws and couldn't retrieve the cooked carcass. A ranger saw a snow-caked bi-

son with an enormous chunk of ice frozen to its beard. The ice fell off and later the ranger hefted it and estimated that it weighed 30 pounds.

Another ranger watched a herd of bison mill around the body of a calf that had died. After a while they filed by the fallen calf, some seemingly paying their last respects by nuzzling the body as they passed. When they had moved out of the area the waiting coyotes moved in.

Carrion such as that bison calf gives life to coyotes, ravens, and, in the spring, emerging grizzlies. Such reminders of nature's pattern—that without death there can be no life—come often during a Yellowstone winter. The deaths of old and sick animals and unfit young ones are part of the culling process that keeps species robust. To see this process, to witness wildlife's winter struggle, is to understand wildlife more fully.

Winter doesn't faze the bobcat *(left)* or the coyote *(above),* both of which can run easily on snow to chase down prey. Though it eats mainly rodents, the adaptable coyote can subsist on ants or berries if need be, biding its time until squirrels or mice become abundant again.

Next page: An implacable bison plows through deep snowdrifts. It can sweep away snow with its head and beard to uncover and eat buried grass.

From the darkened prairie marsh come the mutterings of stirring snow geese. As the sun pinks the sky the mutterings grow louder. Soon, full-fledged squawks and honks resound across the dimly gleaming water. More light, more noise, and in a short while the din escalates to the point where it rivals a roaring crowd at a hard-fought football game. Suddenly, the first formation of snow geese takes off, followed by another and another until the composition of the air seems to have changed to one part oxygen, four parts nitrogen, and five parts snow geese. Gawking at the thousands of snow geese can give a gawker a sore neck, but the pleasure outweighs the pain.

The flight of the snow geese is just one of the reasons wildlife lovers are willing to make the trek to J. Clark Salyer National Wildlife Refuge, which stretches along 50 miles of the Souris River from a point near Bantry, North Dakota, to the Canadian border. The refuge creates an oasis of marshland, sandhills, and wooded river bottoms.

For people who want a change from North Dakota's flat, furrowed fields, the refuge's two auto routes and a canoe trail provide ready access to the various habitats. Wildlife watchers also can use two observation towers and a blind set up on a grouse dancing ground.

In addition to the snow geese, which can top 150,000 in the fall of a good year, the marshes host up to 2,000 tundra swans, 10,000 Canada geese, and 150,000 ducks. Just as impressive are the numbers of nesting waterfowl. It's heartening to know that each year at Salyer, up to 18,000 ducks and 800 Canada geese are born and raised. Besides, it's fun to watch the irresistibly cute ducklings and goslings flippering along behind their mothers out on the marshes. The Canada geese young are especially charming because their mothers take them ashore to browse on fresh grass shoots, where the goslings can be seen in all their downy glory.

These thriving broods no doubt would have delighted the man after whom the refuge was named, J. Clark Salyer. Salyer, a government official, was the force behind the creation and expansion of the nationwide refuge system in the 1930s and 1940s. His fierce love of wildlife was legendary. When lumber interests once threatened a proposed refuge, Salyer brashly called up the U.S. attorney general, and chewed him out—a typical instance of Salyer's passion overwhelming his prudence. Salyer was happiest in the field, so it's fitting that he had such a refuge—and not a federal office building—named after him.

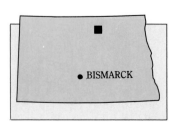

BISMARCK

People who journey to Salyer marvel at both the quantity and variety of waterfowl. Visitors paddling along the canoe trail may spot a radiantly colored wood duck *(below)* or watch the afternoon sky turn dark with the approach of 50,000 snow geese. It's easy to gawk as they flap toward nearby fields to feed, but even a lone goose has its beauty *(left)*. The refuge also abounds in mammals such as beaver, mink, and muskrat.

Visitors can see prairie dogs from the road, but somehow a look at eye level seems more appropriate. Popping out of its hole, the prairie dog *(above)* remains close to the security of its burrow. Prairie dogs and bison *(right)* evoke the feeling of pioneer days, when millions of their kin roamed the plains.

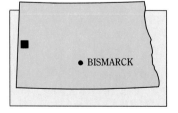

• BISMARCK

At dawn on many spring days, male sharp-tailed grouse turn Roosevelt's prairie knolls into mating grounds, strutting and booming to attract mates *(left)* and repel threatening rivals.

If Theodore Roosevelt hadn't gone in 1883 to the area in North Dakota that is now Theodore Roosevelt National Park, conservation in America might not have blossomed as it did under his presidential guidance. He fell in love with the rough country of the Little Missouri River badlands and bought a ranch, where he stayed on and off for a dozen years. Amid those grasslands and hills, T.R. developed the passionate respect for nature that impelled him to become one of the most powerful conservationists in American history.

Knowing the effect of the area on T.R., one would expect something monumental, such as Yosemite or Yellowstone, but Theodore Roosevelt National Park isn't nearly that grand. Instead, it offers unpretentious grasslands and sagedotted flats, ravines thick with ash and chokecherry, twisted junipers clinging to rocky slopes, and the narrow but lush greenbelt of the Little Missouri River. The park is not flashy, but outdoors people can appreciate a hillside covered with waving western wheatgrass as well as a stand of towering redwoods. And they can appreciate prairie dogs and jackrabbits as well as grizzly bears and timber wolves.

While Roosevelt has its glamour animals (bison, elk, pronghorn, and bighorn sheep) it also harbors species that are integral to the mosaic of prairie life that so intrigued T.R. Coyotes, for example, often are ignored—or despised as varmints—but they're wonderfully resilient hunters that can make do with whatever's available. Watching a coyote "mousing" is a treat. The coyote will sniff around in the dense grass, catch the scent of a mouse or vole, freeze until it hears the little rodent, then launch into the air like a diver off a springboard and knife snout-first into the grass after its prey.

The sharp-tailed grouse is a mottled, brownish bird that few people would glance at a second time, but in spring the males stage courtship displays that are real showstoppers. Dozens of the possessed dancers leap into the air, flash their wings, and do the Muhammed Ali shuffle. They also face off and dance at each other, often synchronizing moves as if they were rehearsing a Broadway musical.

Roosevelt park is a place to reflect on the worth of all natural things, a place to feel the power behind small creatures like the western meadowlark. To T.R., its tremulous, flutelike call evoked ". . . dim hills reddening in the dawn, with the breath of cool morning winds blowing across lowly plains, with the scent of flowers on the sunlit prairie." Today, amid the sagebrush and sunflowers, the western meadowlark still sings in Theodore Roosevelt National Park.

The prairie. It's not just another landscape, not to most Americans. Among the dancing grasses and muscular hills lie cultural memories that have passed into legend, memories of pioneers and scouts and cowboys, of wagon trains and sod houses and cattle drives, of Indian skirmishes and buffalo massacres and range wars. These pioneer and prairie memories are integral to our national identity—and integral to the prairie is prairie wildlife.

It's difficult to imagine a frontier scene without a bison, a rattlesnake, or a prairie dog in the picture, or at least a coyote howling in the background. Sadly, in most parts of the American prairie the animals must be imagined because they're gone: exterminated or crowded out. With a few exceptions, such as the defiantly adaptable coyote, which has prospered, prairie wildlife populations have been grievously reduced over the years by relentless hunting, trapping, poisoning, and destruction of habitat. However, pockets of largely natural prairie do exist, and one of the best for viewing wildlife lies in the southwest corner of South Dakota. It's a combination of two adjoining units of public land: Wind Cave National Park and Custer State Park.

The territory isn't pure prairie because the Black Hills elevate the western sections of the parks, but about 40 percent of the parks' roughly 100,000 acres does consist of hilly mixed-grass prairie. Wildlife watchers shouldn't mind the presence of the ponderosa-pine-studded mountains, though; they're scenic and they spice up the Wind Cave/Custer stew with a hearty dash of species such as mountain goats, elk, and bighorn sheep. The Black Hills insinuate themselves into the grasslands via woodland ravines cut by winding creeks, creating another ecosystem in addition to the prairie and forest. These relatively lush ravines shelter life usually found far to the east, such as eastern bluebirds and bur oaks. However appealing the ravines or the forest might be, the essence of Wind Cave is found atop some low, treeless ridge where a light breeze tousles the grass and the sun-drenched blue grama and western wheatgrass fill the air with the earthy smell of toasted straw.

The king of the prairie is the bison. From 1,000 to 1,300 of these massive creatures live in Wind Cave/Custer, the largest wild population in the United States except for Yellowstone's. Though humankind very nearly annihilated the bison, reducing its numbers from as many as 60 million to mere hundreds by the turn of the century, we will never be more than usurpers in the bison's realm.

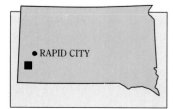

● RAPID CITY

Wind Cave is two parks in one, a cool limestone cave below ground and a paradise for wildlife watchers above. Rolling hills and grassland *(below)* nurture shaggy bison, prairie dogs, and pronghorns *(left)*, which use their excellent eyesight to good advantage on this windswept land.

Hikers in Wind Cave/Custer had better treat bison with deference: bison bulls stand six feet at the shoulder, weigh up to a ton, and wield 20-inch horns. Despite their bulk, they can thunder across the prairie at 35 miles an hour. A wildlife biologist from the east coast who went to Wind Cave to do research initially regarded bison as nothing more than "big cows," but the first snorting assault changed that perception in a hurry. He reckons that over the years in Wind Cave he has been charged by bison about 50 times. No wonder savvy frontiersmen feared bison more than they feared grizzlies.

Bison aren't a menace to humans alone; during the mating season in mid-summer, bulls often battle over cows. Rita Summers, a wildlife photographer who frequents Wind Cave, says, "Bison sometimes lower their heads and really go at each other. They butt heads, back off, then butt heads again, and just keep on banging." Occasionally they will hook each other with those wicked horns. Park rangers find the carcasses of several goring victims every year. The rut also compels the bulls to bellow, a monumental sound that befits their size. Says Summers: "It sounds like lions roaring. You can hear it for miles."

Of course, bison don't generally spend their time bellowing, pawing the turf, or slamming into each other. More often they graze peacefully, stroll to waterholes or mineral licks, rest, and wallow in the dust, doing nothing more aggressive than chewing their cuds. But bison don't have to engage in spectacular behavior to command attention; their very presence is enough. More than any other creature they symbolize the prairie of 150 years ago. They even look like the Wind Cave/Custer prairie, their massive humped contours echoing the hills they roam.

Considerably less regal than the bison but still vital to the prairie is the prairie dog. Prairie dogs live in communities called dog towns, some of them sprawling over hundreds of acres each. Before the prairie dog population was decimated, prairie dogs used to congregate in metropolises that covered thousands of acres. Regardless of their size, dog towns always seem large because they're so crowded and hectic. With prairie dogs scampering about and popping in and out of holes, dog towns look like bustling downtown business districts.

Chubby, slow, and without weaponry to speak of, prairie dogs appear to be easy pickings for an array of able hunters. But appearances can be deceiving. For example, a coyote looking for fast food often will single out a prairie dog that isn't alert and stalk it, but when the coyote gets within about 50 feet of its intended victim, nearby prairie dogs start calling. Instantly, all the prairie dogs in the vicinity scurry to the mounds around their burrows and suspiciously eye the coyote. If the coyote charges a prairie dog, it will dive into its burrow with a waggle of its stubby tail and stay there while the coyote waits futilely above. This pattern may be repeated several dozen times before the disconsolate—and hungry—coyote slouches away. John Hoogland, an associate professor at the University of Maryland who studied prairie dogs at Wind Cave over several years, says that he has seen about 200 coyotes go after prairie dogs, some spending up to 20 minutes in the attempt, and that only two were successful.

Wind Cave's park research biologist, Rich Klukas, says that at other dog towns, particularly those rimmed with tall grass that coyotes can use for cover, coyotes maintain much higher batting averages. Klukas also has seen coyotes nab prairie dogs by stealing into a dog town before dawn, hugging the ground in a shallow depression, and, come morning, pouncing on the first unsuspecting prairie dog that strays within striking distance. Klukas has watched bobcats exercise even greater patience. A bobcat will sneak into a dog town before dawn, stretch out beside the entrance to a burrow, cup its forepaws around the hole, and wait, minutes on end, until an unfortunate prairie dog pokes its head out.

Social behavior among prairie dogs isn't limited to their alarm system. They sound as many as 10 different calls, some of them often, so the dog-town air is noisy with chirps and squawks. There's also a lot of nonvocal behavior going on, particularly within kinship groups called coteries. Members of the same coterie groom each other, loll atop one another, fight against intruders from other coteries, and "kiss," a recognition behavior that sometimes looks like the Europeans' custom of kissing first one cheek and then the other.

Perhaps the most entertaining prairie dog routine is still not completely understood by scientists. Hoogland calls it the "jump-yip display." It looks something like this: a prairie dog that is on all fours or crouching suddenly will shoot to its back feet, fling its front feet above its head and stretch them skyward as if beseeching the heavens. As it unfolds upwards it lets loose a piercing whistle. This whole motion takes about a second and is repeated over and over. Hoogland says it's often an all-clear signal but that it also seems to serve as a territorial call. Sometimes other prairie dogs get into the act until dozens are busily engaged in what looks like rodent aerobics.

To move from the prairie dog to the pronghorn is to

Stretched high, a prairie dog whistles an all-clear signal to other prairie dogs in a South Dakota prairie dog town.

move from the comical to the sublime. Traditionally called the pronghorn antelope, pronghorns are not true antelopes. They've been linked to both goats and cattle. However, anyone who sees a pronghorn will side with the traditionalists, because these swift, graceful, elegantly marked animals evoke images of gazelles, not goats or guernseys.

Pronghorns are born to the prairie. With their powerful vision, they can spot distant predators on the open terrain. They even sport extremely long eyelashes that shade their telescopic eyes for better viewing. The radiantly white hairs on a pronghorn's rump can be held erect to catch the bright prairie sunlight, which produces a brilliant flash that serves as an alarm signal, visible for miles.

But the main reason they thrive on prairies is their speed. Pronghorns are the fastest land mammals in North America and when they're serious they can bound across the tawny prairie grass in 20-foot leaps at 60 miles an hour. Watching a pronghorn run makes us humans feel clumsy and slow, much the same way that watching a falcon fly makes us feel regretfully earthbound.

Despite the pronghorns' speed and eyesight, the prairie dogs' alarm system, and the bisons' intimidating nature, these animals and most other Wind Cave/Custer wildlife can be safely and readily seen. In fact, the open landscape and the relatively small size of the parks allow motorists to see much of the wildlife from their cars. Driving from Wind Cave's main north entrance to the campground one evening, a distance of fewer than 10 miles, I came across one small herd of bison and perhaps half a dozen solitary bulls, including one that passed within five feet of me. (Believe me, I stayed inside my stopped car.) I saw half a dozen wild turkeys; twice I encountered small groups of mule deer, including three that blocked the road and came up to sniff my car; I saw hundreds of prairie dogs and, though I didn't see them, I heard elk bugling and coyotes yipping.

There is one drawback: since plenty of animals can be observed from the road, many people never set foot on the prairie, which is a shame. The mythical quality of the prairie won't come through if the engine's running and the car stereo is playing. Better to leave the car, hike a mile or two, stake out a hilltop, and absorb the aura of the prairie. Listen to the grass whispering in the wind and the coyotes howling. Feel the clean spaciousness, the vastness. Then when a pronghorn springs into view or a herd of bison rumbles along a distant ridge, it will be clear why the prairie is the stuff of legends.

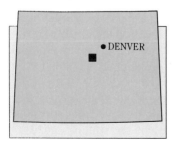

Mountain goats *(right)* are so at home on Mt. Evans that an early morning visitor is likely to spot one, sometimes even snoozing on the sun-warmed highway. Insulated by coats of long outer fur and thick underfur, they are superbly adapted to mountain winters. During the spring mating season, the loud, hooting calls of displaying male blue grouse *(above)* often are heard.

● DENVER

A little effort goes a long way on Mt. Evans. Not only do visitors to the 14,264-foot summit get an elevated view of the Colorado Rockies, but on the drive up they pass through a hotbed of wildlife, the Mt. Evans Wilderness Area. Elk, bears, bighorn sheep, mountain goats, ptarmigan, blue grouse, weasels, pikas, and marmots call the area home, and many of them live so close to the road that they can be watched from the car. In fact, mountain goats sometimes sleep overnight on the blacktop for its warmth, so early-bird motorists must be careful not to hit them—not that any sane driver would speed on this precipitous road.

Which animals visitors see depends largely on where they choose to pull off the road. In the 28 miles from Idaho Springs to Mt. Evans, this road, the highest paved road in America, gains nearly 7,000 feet in altitude, winding from the forest of ponderosa pines and Douglas firs to the treeless expanse of the high tundra. It's up there, on the steep slopes, that Mt. Evans' numerous mountain goats wander.

Odd-looking beasts that they are, mountain goats are entertaining even when they're just standing around. Their behavior makes them absolutely fascinating. The kids put on a great show, running and jumping and practicing their climbing skills. Instead of playing, adults sometimes do serious battle. Says photographer Charles Summers, "Watch for males fighting. They stand beside each other head-to-tail and spin, trying to hook the other goat in the flank with their horns." However, even a knock-down-drag-out fight gets second billing when compared with the sight of a mountain goat doing what it does best: climbing.

Mountain goats are unsurpassed climbers. They can waltz up potentially lethal grades with an ease that stems from a multitude of adaptations, such as their low center of gravity and hooves that are large, squarish, and have a firm edge but a rubbery inner pad, much like climbing shoes.

In his engaging book, *A Beast the Color of Winter,* Douglas Chadwick tells of an intrepid mountain goat that he saw edging along a dwindling cliff edge. The ledge eventually petered out, and it was so narrow that the goat couldn't turn around or even look over its shoulder to back up. The goat shuffled around, seemingly trapped. Then, like a gymnast, it placed its front hooves on the ledge, eased its rear end off the ground, slowly swung its back legs up and over its head while rolling its hindquarters, cartwheeled down to the ledge facing the way it had come, and ambled away. Now, if that doesn't make mountain goats "King of the Mountain," nothing can.

Above the tree line, plant cover is only inches high, and the wind lashes at your skin. Despite the harshness of tundra life during much of the year, yellow-bellied marmots *(right)* eat enough to build up a layer of fat to see them through winter.

● DENVER

Land of no trees. That's what the Russian word *tundra* means, but even so evocative a phrase doesn't prepare visitors to Colorado's Rocky Mountain National Park for the exotic world that awaits them above the tree line. Hiking along a ridge at 13,000 feet, it seems as if the tundra belongs to the sky as much as to the earth. With no trees, and few plants that reach past the tops of a hiker's boots, the tundra is an exhilarating blend of light and space.

The tundra sections—about a third of the park—are a prime cut of the most accessible tundra landscape this side of Alaska. Not only do many moderately easy trails lead above the timberline, but a paved highway, Trail Ridge Road, takes motorists to a high point of 12,183 feet. From vantage points along Trail Ridge the panorama reaches out 50 miles southwest to the Gore Range, 60 miles north to Wyoming's Medicine Bow Mountains, and 30 miles east to the patchwork fields of the Great Plains.

Unfortunately, too many people stop for a snapshot and then drive on, uninterested in the tundra except for the vistas it affords. Admittedly, it is a harsh land, subject to vicious cold, buried under snow for most of the year, and blasted by winds that at their worst have gone off the scale somewhere above 200 mph. But if life can adapt to the black depths of the oceans and to the fiery sands of the Sahara, it can take root in the tundra—and so it has. A close study reveals an ecosystem that is rich, fascinating, and surprisingly fragile.

Tundra plants crumple easily beneath human intrusion. It's as if they were expending every bit of their strength to withstand the natural tribulations of their home and had none left to defend themselves against unnatural threats. When trampled severely, tundra flora can take hundreds of years to recover, so certain areas near parking pulloffs along Trail Ridge have been closed. Fortunately, most tundra areas are used sparingly and remain open, but it helps if hikers observe a few simple rules, such as spreading out instead of walking single file (unless there's already a trail) and walking on rocks.

A summer afternoon's vigil on the tundra offers a glimpse of life in the land above the trees. A shrill, metallic whistle from the talus slope below signals the presence of a pika, a winsome creature that resembles a guinea pig but actually belongs to the same order as rabbits. Pikas lack skyscraping jackrabbit ears, in part because they can't afford the heat loss. Pikas spend much of their day harvesting vegetation and gathering it into "hay piles" for winter use.

Pikas aren't the only whistlers on the tundra. Yellow-

A pika *(left)* sunbathes on the scree slopes, undaunted by the upcoming winter. To prepare for cold weather, the pika collects grass, spreads it out to cure, then shoves it into piles. It must eat from the haystacks almost hourly to get enough energy to withstand the cold.

bellied marmots can be spotted perching on boulders and playing selections from their six-whistle repertoire. These pudgy rodents lead a Life-of-Riley existence that consists of eating, sunning, and sleeping—not to mention their six-to-nine-month hibernation. It's no wonder they often weigh more than 10 pounds and look like mounds of fur with eyes.

Like the pika and the marmot, the white-tailed ptarmigan lives year-round on the tundra, where the frigid weather probably seems balmy to this bird whose kin are commonly found in northern Canada and Alaska. Though they're about the size of pigeons, ptarmigan are tough to spot because they're masters of camouflage. They sport white coats during winter, mottled brown ones during summer, and a blend during the spring and fall when the tundra also is changing colors.

Ptarmigan need their camouflage, just as pikas and marmots need their alarm whistles, because able predators patrol the tundra. Four-legged threats include coyotes, martens, and the voracious long-tailed weasel, which daily can consume prey equal to one-third of its body weight. Northern harriers, prairie falcons, and red-tailed hawks sweep the skies.

Seemingly up there with the birds of prey are the bighorn sheep, which like to hang out on ridgelines or steep slopes. Bighorns surely deserve the overused adjective "majestic." Mature males can weigh 300 pounds, stand 3 feet at the shoulder, and, of course, are crowned by those wonderful, spiraling horns. To see a ram muscle up a precipitous hillside and stand against the blue sky at the top is to see the ultimate symbol of the high country. The locals couldn't agree more; the bighorn is the semi-official symbol of the park and the state mammal of Colorado.

The image most people carry of the bighorn is that of two males butting heads. (They're not called "rams" for nothing.) Anyone who has seen one of those explosive collisions or heard the resounding *whomp* must wonder why rams don't stumble around with permanent concussions. Perhaps they would if their skulls didn't have two layers of bone, reinforced to withstand concussion, and if they weren't protected by those massive horns. In fact, those horns help prevent injury in an even more effective way. The size of the horns largely determines the hierarchy within bighorn bands, so a ram with bigger horns usually gets his way—without a fight—over a ram with smaller horns.

A ram's horn size also reveals its age. The horns grow continually from the base. So a 4-year-old ram will have horns that are just beginning to curl, and a 10-year-old will have a

A few hours' walk can take you from the land-of-no-trees down to dark green forests that appeal to deer *(above)*, elk *(right)*, and hikers alike. Only two hours from Denver, the Rocky Mountain park boasts more than 300 miles of trails that often wind in and around such sylvan settings. Among the sights: curious fawns of mule deer *(below)*, which usually spend their summers in the high mountain meadows.

curl that's coming around full circle. Since the horns aren't shed, observers who focus 20-power spotting scopes on them may even be able to see the annual growth rings.

The rams' horns might be seen only in the park's visitors' centers if it hadn't been for some successful bighorn management during the past few decades. The park's bighorn population was decimated by overhunting, competition from domestic livestock, a shrinking range, and devastating diseases that had been passed on from domestic sheep. The number of bighorns plunged to fewer than 200 by the 1950s, but wildlife managers fought back by ensuring that sheep had access to mineral licks, by reintroducing some sheep, and by phasing out the grazing of domestic sheep on lands next to the park where they had mingled with bighorns. The bighorns are now on the comeback and about 450 sheep live in the park. But they are still vulnerable, even to well-meaning human visitors.

Park biologist Dave Stevens says that when visitors with cameras chase the sheep to get close-up photos, it disrupts the animals' routine and creates stress that can tip the balance, causing the death of a weakened sheep that otherwise would have survived. Stevens' advice: use a telephoto lens—and common sense.

Though most visitors eventually fall for the tundra's spare charm, sooner or later something prompts them to descend to the forest. Perhaps an afternoon lightning storm, or one of the snow showers that can whiten the high country at any time. (Snow almost always closes Trail Ridge Road for at least one day a month, even during July and August.) On the positive side is the temptation of a beautiful lake down below or an inviting meadow beaded with wildflowers. Or maybe human curiosity will assert its pull.

On a recent September sojourn, I spotted some elk moving off the tundra and I certainly would have followed them—had a 500-foot cliff not separated us. The haggard bull and his harem of seven cows were heading to lower pastures, a move probably triggered by the ominous cold front blowing in. The bull trotted back and forth after drifting cows, working like a sheepdog to keep them together. Every minute or so the bull stopped and bugled at something behind him. Scanning the country upslope from the bull, I spied the apparent reason for his bugling: two younger bulls that were tagging along. They may have been interlopers trying to horn in on the older bull's action or young bulls that only recently had gone out on their own and whose mothers were in the harem. Whatever their intent, they aroused consternation in the older bull.

Visitors often spot Steller's jay *(above)* gracing the Rockies' forests. A bold, raucous bird, it sometimes steals food from the acorn woodpecker's cache.

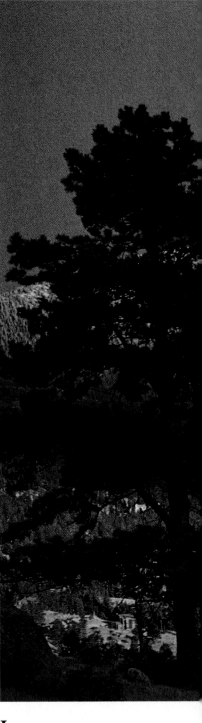

Impressive beyond telling is the view after an afternoon shower *(above),* where earth and sky meet in a rainbow poised over the mountain range. Hikers like Rocky Mountain park for its challenging slopes and hospitable valleys, but such a view makes the journey worthwhile for even the most hardened city-dweller.

Even if nothing so engrossing as an elk melodrama comes up, visitors shouldn't neglect the lower two-thirds of the park. The park's forests are splendid: stands of fir, spruce, pine, and aspen; icy-fresh snowmelt streams; infant rivers bound east and west from their sources near the Continental Divide; sunny meadows, waterfalls, and the famed lakes (Dream Lake, Lake of Glass, Azure Lake, and dozens more, all of which live up to their postcard-perfect names).

Naturally, such a slice of Eden has its full complement of animals. Four or five species of squirrels inhabit the park, but only one of those species caused an excited visitor to come up to ranger-naturalist Leigh Zahn last year and report his sighting: a black rabbit that could, amazingly, climb trees. Suppressing a smile, Zahn politely told the man that he'd seen an Abert's squirrel, which in the park are often black and sport long tufts of hair sticking up from their long, pointy ears.

Hikers also may spot mule deer, which look positively dainty compared to the massive elk. Porcupines and snowshoe hares might be rustling across the floor of pine needles, scooting for safety if they're startled. Sometimes one of the park's ubiquitous coyotes is in pursuit of one of those hares, but sometimes the hunter is a mountain lion or red fox.

Unless a hiker is immersed in the trees, however, the mountains are always visible, forming a towering backdrop that intensifies the beauty of everything set against it. But most of all, the high country makes the park seem purely wild. Its imposing lack of civilization and its glorious inhospitableness make it clear that Rocky Mountain National Park is the realm of the pika, the golden eagle, the elk, and the bighorn, and that we are merely guests.

THE MIDWEST

Preceding page: Threatened by a coming storm, the late afternoon sun shines through the blustery sky over a forested area of Agassiz. Woodlands wildlife is only part of the refuge's variety, which includes abundant marsh animals.

The wind moaned around the refuge headquarters and slush ice crept slowly toward the open heart of the big pools. Tundra swans and hardy mallards stirred uneasily in the cold, choppy water. Winter was scratching at the door. I huddled into a down vest and squinted against gritty snow, blowing almost horizontally. Wildlife viewing paradise? Maybe for musk ox fans. We'd see.

I was waiting to tour Agassiz National Wildlife Refuge with Jim Mattson, refuge biologist. Agassiz, in northwest Minnesota, is a first stop for many species migrating from Canada, fleeing south ahead of winter's anger. It is the mouth of a natural funnel from the sub-Arctic, and from here huge numbers of migrating birds debouch toward the south in the fall and gather to rest in the spring before heading north. Agassiz is so far removed from any population center that you don't happen on it—you *intend* to visit.

The countryside around the refuge would tend to prove the flat earth theory. Once it was a vast prairie, interspersed with small woodlands that pioneered from the great forest to the east. Now it is cropland with potholes drained and prairie plowed, dreary on a flat winter day and without drama.

Then there is Agassiz.

Agassiz covers more than 61,000 acres, most of which is marsh (including a 4,000-acre spruce-tamarack forest). Here you'll find woodland creatures and prairie creatures almost cheek-by-jowl (or, in some cases, fang to throat). Sharp-tailed grouse may be dancing on their spring leks while a pack of timber wolves lingers nearby. Sandhill cranes and up to 25,000 Franklin's gulls nest on the refuge.

I stopped first at an observation tower, leaned into a cutting wind, and watched several ducks pitch into the cattails, which clattered like venetian blinds. Most migratory birds were long gone, and the residents were gearing up for a bitter winter. (Nearby Thief River Falls often logs in with the coldest temperature in the lower 48 states.) In spring, however, these largely empty pools would be covered with squawking, preening, displaying ducks.

Mattson and I drove along a marsh road between a billowing sea of phragmites and a carpet of cattails. As we bounced around in a government-issue pickup truck, we were talking about hunting gray partridge when, by curious coincidence, a covey of them walked out in the road and milled there, reluctant to fly.

If Bill Blass had designed a bird, it would be a gray partridge, the trimmest, neatest, and most color-coordinated of

MINNEAPOLIS

A mink *(left)* sits atop a beaver's cache of twigs to scan for prey. A favorite food is muskrat, which lives in a mound of woven grass *(below)* with underwater entrances.

They look as if they're straight out of a Gary Larson cartoon, but these young coots are for real. Hatched among Agassiz's marsh grasses, the coots display the large lobed feet which are typical of their species and help them swim and dive.

Next page: A contingent of white pelicans bobs and twists in a preening session on a rocky Agassiz shore. Much of the rest of their time is spent soaring on widespread wings, swimming buoyantly, and scooping up fish with their huge yellow bills.

birds. Where a pheasant is gaudy and brash, gray partridges are sleek and cool, Fifth Avenue birds.

We rounded a bend and saw a cow moose browsing on tender willow sprouts. A little later, we came upon a lanky yearling cow ambling down the middle of the road, all ears and legs. She looked like a gawky teenager waiting for someone—anyone—to ask her to the prom. Of all the wildlife at Agassiz, moose are the most dramatic; an estimated 250 of the big animals lived on the refuge in 1988. Your best bet for seeing one is early in the morning or near sunset.

We visited a trap site where refuge personnel fire a rocket net over baited ducks and band them. "Sometimes we catch over 500 at a shot," Mattson said. Rocket nets make it easier to capture wildlife, either to study or to move them from one place to another for management purposes.

Agassiz is named for Louis Agassiz, a pioneer geologist who documented the glacial ice that covered much of northern North America in prehistoric times. The two huge Red lakes, Lake of the Woods, and Mud Lake are among the nearby remnants of that ancient glacier.

Mud Lake challenged the land-drainers and in 1909 was the focus of one of the most ambitious land-draining projects in history. The project successfully delivered the land from standing water, but the tax burden was so heavy that property owners were threatened with bankruptcy. The state stepped in and paid the bills, claimed the land and later sold it to the federal government. Agassiz was set up as a refuge in 1937.

Joe Kotok has been refuge manager at Agassiz for nearly 20 years and has seen the flat northern landscape change. Until the 1970s, much of the private land around the refuge and its associated state lands was dotted with good marsh, woods, and prairie habitat, but "five dollar wheat made everyone a crop farmer," Kotok said. "By 1975, we'd lost nearly all the historic habitat in northwest Minnesota." Today, Agassiz is an island of wildlife habitat in a sea of intensive farming.

Agassiz is laced with interior roads and trails. The casual drop-in likely will be limited to the auto-tour route across the south end of the refuge. A 100-foot observation tower gives a panorama of Agassiz pool, the refuge's largest, but the tower is not for the acrophobic.

Wildlife blossoms twice during the year, in spring and again in fall. Autumn's color change provides the most attractive backdrop. On the other hand, dancing cranes and grouse decorate the landscape in spring, and birds are at their most colorful then. Yellow-headed and red-winged blackbirds fill the marsh with their calls and splash color on the greening cattails.

In June and July, shorebirds and waterbirds display their breeding plumage. Earlier in the spring and late in the fall, migrating waterfowl, including tundra swans and various geese, abound. Stately white pelicans form bright armadas on the wind-ruffled pools in the summer.

On our short tour, Jim and I saw a great horned owl, a covey of gray partridge, two moose, tundra swans, a variety of ducks, muskrat, snow buntings, tree sparrows, and magpies. We also saw an eagle, now caught by the wind and sailing like a kite, now fighting against it. I wondered at the bitterness that must be the winter here.

Humans enjoy limited use of Agassiz in winter because the blown snow is tough to traverse with skis or showshoes and conditions often are near-arctic. Only the wolves can travel the entire frozen refuge.

One morning, a few years back, Mattson got a report of timber wolves in a grassland on the refuge. He had helped on wolf research near Duluth/Superior, and describes himself as a wolf howler, the way someone else would say, "Yes, I'm a carpenter." It is a skill not in great demand in major cities.

Mattson drove to the field and stopped near a mud puddle with two wolf tracks in it, one big, one little. "I climbed on top of the truck and let out a howl. Nice quiet morning, no wind. Before I finished the second howl, I got an answer. This wolf starts coming and then there's another one and another one and I'm standing on top of my vehicle in plain sight.

"They stop 50 yards away, looking everywhere but up. I'm pretty excited."

Maybe that's why the refuge people stay forever at Agassiz, bitter winters notwithstanding. A few wolves howling in the icy night might put a chill up your backbone, but they kindle a deep warmth in your heart.

The pack of about eight wolves has been resident since 1981 and is the only one on the refuge. Visitors might see them, but they can be elusive. Or they can be oddly unafraid. One refuge worker on a tractor reported that the pack trotted across a field while he was stopped and sat in a semicircle around him, looking solemnly at the noisy mechanical invader.

So, Agassiz may be only a little way from a modern little town, with its fast food restaurants and Rotary luncheons, but when you've howled wolves and watched grunting moose bulldoze their way through the brush, you have gone farther than a few highway miles.

You have leaped across the centuries.

Nickolas Devalk may not grow up with a fondness for the outdoors, but if so, it won't be for lack of exposure to it. He's my grandson and he bobbed in a baby backpack on his father's shoulders as we hiked in the Minnesota Valley National Wildlife Refuge near Minneapolis. Deer had left valentines for us, their heart-shaped hoofprints, and the air was sharp, trees showering gold leaves on the trail. Nickolas wasn't taking it all in—in fact, the sun's warmth and the rhythm of walking had lulled him asleep—but then he was only eight months old. Give him time.

For the rest of us, the hike was a respite from city hustle and bustle. Few urban areas boast as much wildlife as Minneapolis/St. Paul. You wouldn't want to drink the Minnesota River's water untreated, but the meandering valley, subject to floods that keep people projects out, is rich with trumpeter swans, eagles, white pelicans, and ducks. The refuge is a link to the past, reminiscent of how the Dakota Indians must have seen the valley years ago: its river bottoms full of geese and fish, its tree-lined bluffs dotted with bobwhite quail.

Today, the refuge's seven units string out along the Minnesota River for 34 miles. The Black Dog unit, named for a Dakota Indian leader, is dominated by the looming stack of a Northern States power plant whose warm water discharge keeps much of the area free of ice in winter. Yet remarkably, the Black Dog unit contains remnants of prairie land and some rare fen habitat. Fens are peatlands that are saturated with groundwater, and, here in the Minnesota Valley, they are unusually rich in minerals and rare vegetation.

Miles of trails wind throughout the refuge. In spring, you can see male red-winged blackbirds fiercely defending their territories, or watch pileated woodpeckers boring on trees in the bottomlands. Visitors enjoy the area year-round, with the possible exception of summer (the state bird is alleged to be The Mosquito); winter is superb for cross-country skiers.

On our hike, Nickolas woke in the bright October sun and rubbed his eyes. A pair of mallards whispered overhead, and he craned his neck to see them. I clambered up a berm at the perimeter of the wildlife area—and looked down on a gravel pit full of bustling dump trucks. It was a reminder of the city and its two million residents, just a few minutes away. The refuge headquarters is not far from the Minneapolis airport and great jets compete with Canada geese to see which can make the smoothest landing. Grain elevators and barges can be seen from along the riverbank. All the trappings of modern urban life are here, yet the setting is thankfully wild.

MINNEAPOLIS

Minneapolis/St. Paul is one of the few urban areas to boast a great quantity and variety of wildlife, thanks in part to the Minnesota Valley refuge *(below).* Among resident animals is a variety of owls. One of the smaller kinds is the saw-whet *(left),* whose mellow call is repeated throughout the night.

If the Platte River weren't there, sandhill cranes would have to invent it—or there wouldn't be any sandhill cranes. Meandering through central Nebraska, the Platte River is vital to the spring migration of more than half a million sandhills. It is the midpoint of the sandhill crane migration, a place for the cranes to rest and feed on their long journey north to nesting areas in Canada, Siberia, and Alaska.

And it is here where bird enthusiasts migrate each spring to watch the cranes—up to 20,000 of them per mile along the "Big Bend" stretch of the Platte River. It is the largest concentration of cranes in the world.

Cranes aloft resemble nothing so much as sleek jets, their flight lines wavering and throbbing against colorful midwestern sunsets. Cranes landing are the Concordes of the bird world, stick-like legs extended, wings cupped slightly on a long glide to a chosen sandbar.

Nothing on earth sounds like a sandhill crane and nothing in our galaxy sounds like half a million sandhill cranes. Outdoor writer Charley Waterman has called the sound "a musical ratchet." It's somewhat like the noise made by a small boy dragging a stick along a picket fence, a cricketlike chirrup. But multiplied many thousand-fold it is an undulating, rolling wild sound that makes the little hairs on the back of your neck spring to attention.

The cranes begin to gather in mid-February and their numbers peak in mid-March. About two-thirds of the crane population finds refuge in the stretch between Kearney and Grand Island, Nebraska. You can spot cranes in farm fields any time of day (more work the south side of the river than the north), but the huge flights are at dusk and dawn. Each evening, the cranes come back to the Platte from a day of feeding nearby. The big birds vacuum up waste grain (high protein chow to fuel their avian engines) and invertebrates that they find in the wet meadows along the river. Cranes need the Platte and its rich invertebrate life, a source of calcium that serves them well at egg-laying time far to the north.

While local crane enthusiasts abound, some residents pay no more attention to the birds than we do to a flock of blackbirds. Many wonder what all the fuss is about when local motels fill up with crane watchers, wearing down coats against the chill of dawn, their necks draped with binoculars, the telltale lavalier of the birdwatcher.

It's tough to get close to a sandhill crane. They're wary and sharp-eyed. Some photographers seeking crane closeups dig a pit and crouch in the dank ground for hours, hoping a

In spring, the Platte River teems with sandhill cranes in transit to nesting areas in Canada and Alaska. Half a million sandhills stop on the Platte's inviting sandbars, with the vast majority of the birds concentrated in the section known as the "Big Bend."

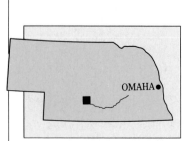

OMAHA

Sandhills, their bright carmine foreheads flashing in the sun *(right)*, spend the day in the fields and wet meadows along the river. There they feed on waste grain and on invertebrates they find along the banks. Aloft *(far right)*, a crane may cut an elegant figure or a comical one.

crane will land nearby for a portrait sitting. An alternative is to crawl along a fencerow across sandburs, hoping to sneak close enough for frame-filling photos.

The problem with any bird is that, no matter how large, it isn't large enough to fill a photo frame unless you're very close or have a telephoto lens. The closest I was able to sneak to cranes was in a slimy pig yard, not exactly pristine surroundings. Another time, I slithered on my belly for about 200 yards in a furrow just across from a flock of cranes. I figured to get within perhaps 30 yards, cautiously poke a 200mm lens through the grass, and take some dynamite wildlife shots.

But cranes are almost telepathic in their ability to sense intruders. After a carpet of vicious little sandburs had destroyed the elbows of my sweater, not to mention the skin on my elbows, I roused up, peeked through the grass, and found the cranes had moved exactly as far from me as the distance I had laboriously crept along.

If a field is 100 acres, you can bet any cranes in it will be equidistant from the fences around it. Canny crane watchers use spotting scopes or good binoculars.

Cranes mostly stand around, but if they begin to "dance" it's a new ball game. The birds leap into the air in gyrations that resemble what Ray Bolger looks like as the Scarecrow in the *Wizard of Oz.*

A sandhill crane stands about three feet high and looks like a feathered arrow in flight. If you're lucky to get eyeball to eyeball with one, you'll find it has the suspicious glare of a loan shark, a yellow eye that doesn't believe anything. The adults have a red crown but the rest of the bird is gray. Sandhills are all legs, their long black stilts allowing them to wade around in the shallow Platte without getting their bodies wet.

Crane country is at the breakover point between the corn and bean land of the midwest and the sweeping billow of the great prairie. The Platte carries a stream of life across Nebraska, nurturing a green belt on either side of its muddy banks for 310 miles.

Once, the Platte was characterized as "a mile wide and an inch deep." The changes from that historic Platte are staggering. While the Platte may be the lifeblood to the cranes, the cranes don't have much political clout and so their river has been divvied up by people. Much of the Platte's annual flow never makes it to the crane resting areas because dams and management projects divert it to agriculture and other uses. The flows also are regulated so that they are more stable, which has allowed trees to grow along the river banks. Cranes prefer a wide channel with no vegetative bottlenecks, yet in the new setting, unfortunately, the flock is constricted. The environmental changes make for a more dramatic gathering, but the concentration around Kearney causes crane enthusiasts to worry.

What the changes in the Platte will mean to the cranes in the long run is probably not good. Crowding leads to problems, such as avian diseases. But for the moment the cranes will drift through the sunsets to their evening rest and those who appreciate them will savor the moment.

The river can be a maze of channels that skirt islands or, in some cases, putter off into nowhere. Some people canoe the Platte. You can spend a lot of time dragging the canoe because the river is one big sandbar. Yet it's a delight to picnic or camp on, and just remember that clean sandbars and ankle-deep water are what the cranes thrive on.

While the Platte valley is crane country, it also is host to other migrants and many resident critters. Wild turkeys and deer roam the willow jungles and, at peak migration, Canada geese are almost as numerous as the cranes.

Once I was driving along Interstate 80 near dusk when I glanced into an adjacent field and saw a buck with a rack that either Boone or Crockett would have killed for. The huge stag gazed incuriously at the passing traffic, then was gone in the night behind me. Chances are, President Eisenhower didn't envision I-80 as a wildlife viewing route when he endorsed the interstate highway system, but it serves the purpose.

One evening we stumbled across a lumpy meadow to see the cranes come in to roost. We clambered into an elevated blind, a group of strangers brought together by a common interest. "Wait till you see it!" exclaimed one who'd been here before. The sun lowered and began to put on a pyrotechnic sunset.

The noise was faint at first, a breath of sound that could have been the rising wind. It grew and resolved into an eerie symphony. The birds came in wavering lines, talking incessantly. Flock after flock drifted in to the bars, thousands of big birds doing what they've done for thousands of years. The excited human chatter in the blind abruptly turned into silence.

Quivira/Cheyenne Bottoms boasts wildlife such as the ring-necked pheasant *(right)*. When startled, it bursts into the air with loud squawking and a whirring of wings. Migrating waterfowl also stop at the refuges. Canvasback ducks *(left)* reach peak numbers in late November and early December.

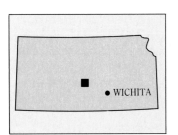

WICHITA

Rare is the area that serves the needs of the shorebird enthusiast and the chicken lover equally well. But a dowitcher devotee can spend his day admiring the stilted legs of shorebirds on the mudflats of Quivira National Wildlife Refuge and his evening 60 miles northeast, munching crisp, plump fryers at the Brookville Hotel.

In south central Kansas, Quivira and the nearby state-owned Cheyenne Bottoms Wildlife Area are to wildlife viewing what the Brookville Hotel is to fried chicken. They effectively refute the claim that Kansas has nothing worth seeing but roads that lead somewhere else. About 90 percent of all the shorebirds in the United States stop at Quivira and Cheyenne Bottoms on their spring and fall migrations. The two places serve as a major link in the chain of refuges down the central flyway from Canada to Texas and Mexico.

The landscape around Quivira can't decide if it wants to be midwest farmland or cowboys-and-Indians country. One minute you're driving along cropfields where it's so flat you could shoot a game of snooker; the next you're in rolling sand-hills where you expect Marshal Dillon to stride over the ridge, sixguns smokin'. This ambivalence carries over into the wild-life you see. Both eastern and western birds meet and mingle. You might see a scissor-tailed flycatcher, a southwestern bird whose tailfeathers are foolishly long, then an eastern bluebird or a chickadee, eastern birds with cowboy ambitions.

Quivira is named for an Indian tribe which, in turn, was named by the Spanish explorer Coronado in 1541. Coronado expected to find real gold; instead he found the golden grasses of the great prairie. Today that prairie harbors yellow-headed blackbirds and golden eagles, at home in their environment.

The refuge is roughly key-shaped, with Big Salt Marsh in the head of the key and Little Salt Marsh in the shank. The two basins hold the water that makes Quivira attractive to migrating birds. Shorebird migration, which hits its prime from the first of May to about the first week of June and again from mid-August through September, includes plovers, avocets, dowitchers, phalaropes, and sandpipers. A dedicated, even feverish, band of bird enthusiasts who specialize in shorebirds comes to watch them here, because few places in America are richer in their collection of long-legged birds.

Waterfowl numbers peak in late November and early December with about 30,000 Canada geese and perhaps 40,000 ducks. That's impressive, but a far cry from what must have existed when the parents of some area oldtimers shot a wagonload of ducks in a day and salted them down for eastern markets. The fabled waterfowl resource also fueled many hunting clubs at the turn of the century.

Both Cheyenne Bottoms and Quivira are temporary homes to migrating whooping cranes, likely to be there in October or November. Whoopers stop in central Kansas almost every year, but usually it is a touchdown stay, a fleeting visit come and gone before the word gets out.

Visitors usually wander the refuge at will. "The only time it ever has been a problem was when a couple of guys got too close to whooping cranes and forced the cranes to leave," explained Jim McCollum, refuge manager at the time. Parts of Quivira are now closed to visitation when whoopers are there.

Quivira also has Kansas' largest breeding colony of least terns, an endangered species.

I once visited in mid-winter, admittedly not the best time for wildlife viewing. A few mallards swam in the salt marsh pools, which were shrunken by prolonged drought. Overhead a red-tailed hawk wheeled in a stiff prairie wind and thousands of acres of tallgrass bent in homage. The sighing wind was eternal, obeying forces bigger than anything humans can muster. I looked over the vast sweep of prairie and wondered, as Coronado did, where my legendary golden cities were.

The refuge was quiet, gripped by cold. It lay patiently, awaiting the spring and a full house. Maybe that was the real treasure, this annual rich flowering of animal life.

An American bittern *(above)* sits motionless with its bill pointed skyward. The bird usually hangs out among the marsh's cattails, where its pose and coloration render it nearly invisible. Only a few days old, a white-tailed fawn *(right)* peeks out from its hiding place in the foot-high yarrow at Quivira refuge.

148

KANSAS CITY

Rising in a mass of flapping wings, mallards *(below)* attract the attention of hungry bald eagles *(left)* at Squaw Creek. Several hundred of the raptors winter at the refuge, perching in trees to watch for crippled waterfowl and other prey.

Maybe you say "low-iss," or is it "lurse" or even "lowss"? However you pronounce "loess," which is wind-deposited, fine-grained soil (and the dictionary accepts both "low-iss" and a gutteral "lerse"), the dark hills that overlook Squaw Creek National Wildlife Refuge in northwest Missouri form a dramatic backdrop for 350,000 snow geese during peak migration.

Snow geese are nicknamed "wavies" for their undulating, irregular flight formations. They talk continually, and in October and November the skies of northwest Missouri are a cacophony of high, alarmed goose gossip.

If geese are the most abundant wildlife, it is the wintering populations of bald eagles that are the most spectacular. In a typical year, Squaw Creek will host up to 300 bald eagles. It's nothing to see half a dozen wheeling over the marsh or perched in gaunt trees. They come to feed on waterfowl crippled by hunting or illness. In winters when the water doesn't freeze solid, the eagles will be around as long as there is something to eat.

In early December the refuge, in cooperation with the Missouri Department of Conservation, sponsors annual Eagle Days, when visitors can see dozens of eagles and learn about them from experts.

Arriving earlier in the fall are pelicans, stand-offish birds that raft in stark-white flotillas as far from the road as they can get. Not so the shorebirds that putter intently on their stilted legs, cartoon birds that ignore everything but a shot at a meal.

The refuge also is rich in resident wildlife, including deer and pheasants. Take a hike on the loess bluff trail overlooking the marsh and enjoy the flocks of snow geese and patches of bluestem and Indian grass. If you squint your eyes just right, you can imagine yourself a member of the Lewis and Clark expedition, seeing a pristine Missouri River valley. When Lewis and Clark passed close by 185 years ago, the sloughs along the river were literally black with waterfowl.

Today, Squaw Creek visitors can still enjoy exceptional wildlife viewing, as well as a bike tour of the refuge in late October that offers brilliant fall color. Once we met friends from St. Joseph and rode the entire refuge road network. Bill and Charlotte Bennett had found a bicycle-built-for-two, while we had a mixture of kids' bicycles and sleek racers. We stopped under a tree where a bald eagle looked down on us with supercilious disdain. Later that afternoon, my kids, then preteenagers, were for once silent, quieted by the sound and sight of thousands of geese gabbling and swirling in flight.

A female Canada goose hovers protectively close to her golden goslings *(above)* on a nest atop a muskrat house. A yellow-headed blackbird perched on the tip of a cattail *(bottom right)* belts out its rhythmic song at daybreak.

Canada geese are the living symbol of wildness. They also are the symbol of the National Wildlife Refuge system, and their chill cries on a sharp early winter night are the audible breath of the world's icebox, far to the north. In few other places is there a greater concentration of Canada geese than at Horicon National Wildlife Refuge in east central Wisconsin. Farmers sometimes call the geese names when thousands of them descend on crop fields, but the names don't sound like "living symbols of wild glory."

Still, for 300,000 to 400,000 human visitors a year, many from Milwaukee or Madison, an hour away, or Chicago, three hours distant, the geese are the reason they're there. About 200,000 geese come in a bumper year, along with 50,000 to 60,000 or more ducks, mostly mallards—waterfowl as they must have been seen by Indians and the first settlers.

The refuge comes to life as the pale wash of predawn lights the frosted crop stubble. The geese are impatient, prattling through their preflight checklist. Then they lift in a hoarse gabble, a roar of hurrying wings. Flocks of mallard ducks whisper overhead, their wings creaking and rushing, a gabby hen seemingly giving directions.

The refuge is part of a 31,000-acre cattail marsh, one of the largest in the United States. The northern two-thirds of the marsh is Horicon National Wildlife Refuge and the southern third belongs to the Wisconsin Department of Natural Resources. Horicon is smack in the middle of the Mississippi Valley flyway, one of the continent's great invisible channels down which migrating waterfowl funnel in the fall to wintering areas in the south. In the spring they fly through again to reach breeding grounds in Canada and the northern United States.

If you're a goose watcher, there is no such thing as too many geese; but to a farmer whose cropfield is black with Canada geese, that's too many geese. It takes nearly a quarter of a million pounds of food daily to fuel a flock of 400,000 birds. Some of that, inevitably, is from crop fields.

The geese arrive at Horicon in mid-September and move on south at freezeup, sometimes as late as the end of December. The Main Dike Road, a major interior road, is open to the public until September 15. After that, goose watching becomes a perimeter sport because of hunters on the scene.

I've spent many a dawn watching geese drop into decoys and even if I weren't hunting, the sight would thrill me. Talking incessantly, the big birds sideslip to lose altitude, set their wings and glide smoothly in, necks stretching for the earth, big black feet extended.

An impressive concentration of Canada geese funnels through Horicon *(above)* in spring and fall. Tuneful honking, which naturalist Aldo Leopold called "goose music," announces their arrival at Horicon, one of the largest freshwater cattail marshes in the United States.

In addition to the geese, about 250 bird species have been spotted on the refuge, as well as the usual assortment of midwest mammals—deer, fox, squirrel, muskrat, raccoon, skunk, mink, river otter, opossum, and coyote.

Horicon is one of the largest nesting areas east of the Mississippi River for redhead ducks, a species whose population has plummeted in recent years. The birds are victims of drought and the draining of their pothole nesting areas. They depend more than ever on Horicon's hospitable acres.

That protective aspect of Horicon offers visitors a peek at history. It is a chance to see wetlands as the settlers saw them, but perhaps with eyes that are more knowing and less interested in change.

A group of white-tailed deer *(right)* and a black bear mother with cubs *(left)* pause in forest clearings as if posing for family portraits. Cubs are usually born in winter and stay with their mothers for a year. It's best to view a female with cubs from a distance because the mother can be a formidable adversary if she feels threatened.

SAGINAW●

Michigan's beautiful Pigeon River Country supports 22 active oil wells, all chugging in counterpoint to the bugling of elk. Oil and elk? As Alice would say so ungrammatically, "curiouser and curiouser." Ah, but elk and oil *do* mix here, and so do oil and water, the kind blue-ribbon trout love to swim in. Pigeon River Country encompasses 165 square miles of Michigan's upper Lower Peninsula (a lovely oxymoron). About 1,200 elk, the largest herd east of the Mississippi River, roam here. Yet wild animals share the forested country with an oil field.

Oil was discovered in 1970, and since then the area has been pulled between oil development and protection of the wildness. This is an area cherished by Michiganders, so the wells are strictly regulated. The elk appreciate the open areas for grazing. From 1981 through 1986, oil and gas royalties kicked $37 million into Michigan's natural resources coffers.

Elk are antlerless in the early spring, but by fall the bulls have a full rack. It's astonishing that an animal as large as a horse can filter through thick woods like ground fog, but elk do it. The quiet woods-walker, if he is lucky, will see a bull elk suddenly appear in a sun-dappled forest opening.

Major wildlife species include the elk, of course, plus deer, bear, bobcat, coyote, ruffed grouse, woodcock, snowshoe hare, pine marten, squirrel, beaver, otter, muskrat, waterfowl, and many songbirds.

It's even possible to sneak up on a grouse "drumming" in the spring. Male birds stand atop a favored fallen log and rapidly beat their wings, without flying off, to establish territory and broadcast the news of their charm to possible mates. The sound is like that of a tractor starting up, a rumbling boom created by the bird's snapping wings.

You can hear the male's percussive wingbeat a long way, and if you move closer each time the bird drums it's possible to get within sight without spooking him.

Besides wildlife watching, Pigeon River Country offers fishing in top-notch trout streams, including Pigeon, Black, and Sturgeon rivers, and deer hunting. Hikers enjoy the High Country and Shingle Mill pathways and a horse trail. Shingle Mill is a good route for elk-gawking and also is maintained for cross-country skiers.

This is northwoods country, home of the black fly and mosquito in summer, but always clean-smelling because of the dense conifer forest.

Ernest Hemingway fished Pigeon River Country as a boy, probably finding solace there from the outside world. Maybe it's the wind soughing through pines or the clean smell of the trees. Maybe it's the dark, cold northern waters, rushing over rounded glacial boulders. Or the soft moss, warm from a summer sun.

There cannot be any place more serene than a smoothly flowing trout stream on a soft, warm day, with a beaver busily trundling building materials like a carpenter, or a river otter sleekly splitting the current.

The Pigeon River area *(below)* attracts people who like to hike, watch wildlife, and fish for trout. Spectacular fall foliage draws visitors in search of beauty and solitude. The resident yellow-bellied sapsucker *(left)* leaves a telltale sign: orderly rows of small holes in trees. Sap oozes into the holes, and the sapsucker laps it up with its brushlike tongue.

THE SOUTHEAST

Preceding page: Sunset finds wading birds returning to roost for the night at Florida's Everglades National Park.

Heading south from Miami, past shopping malls and countless stucco homes, the turnpike narrows and a zig-zagging road veers west through wide fields of tomatoes and squash. Gradually, tile-roofed houses give way to fruit stands advertising homegrown bananas, tree-ripened avocados, and limes. A sign warns travelers: No food, lodging, or fuel next 44 miles.

Ahead, pine forest hugs the right-of-way, and dense shrubs arch in a shady canopy above the road. Beyond this tunnel of green waves a field of golden sawgrass, surveyed by an attentive red-shouldered hawk perched on a sabal palm. In the sun-sparkled water of a nearby pond, an alligator lunges, startling a great egret into flight.

It's only 45 miles from the skyscrapers and freeways of downtown Miami, but the contrast is striking. You've just entered Everglades National Park.

First impressions of the Everglades depend upon the season. From late May through October, billowing thunder-heads and afternoon showers are the rule. Much of the park's 50 inches of annual rain comes in summer deluges, and the muggy air hangs heavy with humidity. In summer, mosquito

Boardwalks like Mahogany Hammock Trail lead modern-day explorers into an exotic tropical forest *(left)*. Alligators *(far left)* prefer the lower areas, which contain water even when the rest of the park is parched.

The Everglades' bogs and waterways host a colorful profusion of life, from a katydid on a grass pink orchid *(above)* to the ubiquitous anhinga. After each fishing foray, the anhinga must assiduously dry and preen its feathers *(right)* before it can fly again. The bird's long, sinuous neck *(top right)* gives it the moniker "snakebird."

reproduction shifts into high gear. Unwary visitors who arrive without insect repellent may later display souvenir bumper stickers with a bold red cross and the plucky slogan "I gave at Everglades National Park."

Winters here are clear, dry, and mild—pleasant weather that beckons visitors from snow country. Falling water levels concentrate fish, frogs, turtles, wading birds, and alligators around deeper pools, so wildlife watching is superb. One of the finest areas is seen from the Anhinga Trail.

Within a few steps, the reason for the boardwalk's name becomes apparent. Anhingas are everywhere! These long-necked fishing birds, locally called "water turkeys," hunt entirely under water. Using its turkey-like tail as a rudder, an anhinga pokes into submerged vegetation searching for bream, small bass, and catfish. When it needs a breath, the hidden anhinga then pops its slender head and neck periscope fashion above the surface.

Under water, anhingas stab their prey with rapier-sharp beaks. To eat, the birds surface. They flip small prey such as minnows high into the air, then catch and swallow it. The act resembles the human showoff at a party, tossing popcorn in the air, then lunging to catch it in his mouth.

A large fish may be so firmly impaled that an anhinga must beat the prize against a rock or tree root to dislodge it. Dripping wet, webbed feet wrapped clumsily around a limb, the anhinga struggles to keep its balance as it looks down its bill at the wiggling fish. After repeatedly bashing its prey, the bird lunges forward and flips the fish into the air. It catches the slippery prey head first, so the spines will slide down easily, and swallows the meal in two or three undulating gulps.

Anhingas are not the only attraction, however. Birds, turtles, and alligators living near the Anhinga Trail seem to know that gawking humans on the boardwalk are not a threat and tolerate the humans' close approach. Yet the animals are definitely wild. Take the day photographer Stan Osolinski watched an American bittern catch a snake. "The bittern had the snake by the tail," Osolinski related. "The snake was striking, and the bird was watching it so intently that it didn't notice an alligator inching closer. In one quick grab, the gator had them both for lunch."

The adjacent Gumbo Limbo Trail, and the Mahogany Hammock Trail farther down the main road, are pathways into tropical forests. Overhead, the West Indian mahogany's gnarled branches nurture the wind-borne seeds of orchids and bromeliads and the tiny spores of resurrection ferns. The bro-

meliads' broad, cup-shaped bases make natural collectors for rainwater. The water not only sustains these plants that have no roots in the soil, but also offers refreshment to insects, attracts tree frogs that dine on the insects, and lures snakes that gobble up the frogs.

Amid this lush aerial garden, tiger-striped daggerwing and dainty zebra butterflies flutter in search of nectar. Below, layers of decomposing leaves create a rich, pungent odor, laced with the skunky smell of stopper, a shrub that thrives in the dappled light of the forest floor.

Moist summer months also bring out scores of colorfully banded tree snails, crawling on smooth-barked trees in search of lichens to eat. Their ancestors, clinging tightly to floating logs, may have been blown from Cuba and Hispañola on waves propelled by hurricane winds. Once here, they dispersed into the forests. During the dry winter, the trunks and branches of tamarind, pigeon plum, and fig are decorated with the snails' rainbow colored shells, cemented firmly to the host tree.

At the end of the main road, the once-prosperous fishing village of Flamingo provides entrance to Florida Bay. About a third of Everglades National Park lies submerged in shallow estuaries punctuated with mangrove-fringed islands called keys. Fish and crustaceans abound here, the staple foods of paddle-beaked roseate spoonbills and rare reddish egrets.

Shorebirds and waders crowd the mud flats of Florida Bay. Binoculars and spotting scopes at the ready, bird-watchers converge near shore at low tide to sort out the multitudes of sandpipers, dowitchers, long-legged herons and egrets. Flocks of wild flamingos from the Bahamas were seen here occasionally around the turn of the century, and from them the village took its name. Disappointed birders learn that incidental flamingos seen now are usually escapees from Miami's zoos and aviaries.

Ospreys, however, offer spectacular air shows. Also known as fish hawks, these large black and white birds will dive into the bay from heights of 70 feet or more to snag a mullet. Bald eagles—an average of 50 pairs—also nest in the park. Sometimes a freeloading eagle will target an osprey. Screaming and waving its formidable talons, the eagle forces the osprey to drop its catch. Then the acrobatic eagle deftly sideslips away to snatch the falling fish before it hits the water.

Water sustains all life in the Everglades. The Everglades watershed—a "river of grass"—fans southwest from Lake Okeechobee, trickling slowly over the flat land, then seeping into the Gulf of Mexico. The main flow entering the park is

Mangrove tree crabs *(above)* and great blue herons *(right)* perch on the branches and dense, arching roots of red mangrove trees. In more open water, a young Florida soft-shelled turtle suns itself on a lily pad *(top right)*.

Shark Slough, 50 miles wide but only inches deep, choked with gently swaying spike rush and jagged-edged sawgrass. Early explorers who sailed small boats into the region were reminded of grassy glades they had known in the Old World. In this wild new land, the grass stretched as far as the eye could see: "forever glades," according to one mapmaker. That is one of many explanations of how the area got its name.

A memorable way to view the river of grass is to ride a tram or bicycle around the 15-mile Shark Valley loop in the heart of the park. Explore early in the morning, when fog lingers over the glades, and you may have the place nearly to yourself. Deer slosh through the sawgrass, and raccoons patter about in the shallows, feeding on insects, frogs, and fish.

Nearby, a park ranger leads fifth graders from Miami on a "slog," or wet hike. Few of the city-dwellers have visited the park before. They follow hesitantly, fearful they will sink into quicksand or be snapped up by giant alligator jaws emerging from the black water.

"It's okay," the ranger coaxes, plunging knee-deep into the slough. "I'm not sinking." One by one, the children follow, giggling as cool water rushes into their hightop tennis shoes.

Their leader passes out dip nets and within minutes the children investigate mosquito fish, a dragonfly nymph, a fat brown crayfish, and three kinds of snails. "This isn't scary like I thought it would be," one girl confides. "It's fun!"

Echoing with the children's laughter is the limpkin's mournful wail, sometimes mistaken for people lost in the swamp. Named for their jerky, tail-flicking gait, the birds dine on freshwater organisms such as apple snails—golf-ball-sized mollusks that live in fresh water.

The apple snails are a favorite of snail kites, too. When the number of apple snails dropped during a drought in the 1960s and early '70s, kite numbers plummeted to about 60 birds. A series of wet seasons allowed apple snails to repopulate, and so did kites, though they are still endangered. Like all Everglades wildlife, snails and kites survive in response to the annual pulse of wet and dry. The problems arise when human demands for water interfere with these natural cycles.

Nearly two million people live within a 75-mile radius of Everglades National Park, making its sanctuary a wild, welcome contrast to the homes and tomato fields that surround it. The land may not be as pristine as it was a century ago, but when a flock of egrets settles into the mangroves or an otter unexpectedly pops out of the sawgrass, one still feels a compelling kinship with the natural world that is the Everglades.

Feeding is an inexact art for a wood stork, which simply dips its open bill into the water, waits until a fish bumps into it *(above),* then snaps it shut in a speedy 1/40th of a second.

FT.
• MYERS

T he sun rose more than an hour ago, but its rays still have not penetrated the thick mist that hangs over Corkscrew Swamp. *Who-who-who-whooall* booms a barred owl. From the distance comes a slow *whooall* reply. The owl ruffles its feathers, tucks one leg close to its breast, and nods sleepily. Another night's hunt is over.

For other animals in this 10,560-acre National Audubon sanctuary, the day is just beginning. The silence is shattered by the drumming cadence of a pileated woodpecker's beak on a hollow snag. The echoes bounce from tree to water and back again. A lone birder, the first of many who will visit Corkscrew on this February morning, tries to pinpoint the sound.

Forty feet up an old baldcypress, a female wood duck peers out. She has claimed an abandoned woodpecker den and is incubating eggs while enjoying the penthouse view of the boardwalk that leads into Corkscrew Swamp.

Corkscrew, northwest of Naples, Florida, protects one of the few remaining tracts of uncut baldcypress. These massive trees—100 feet tall and 400 to 700 years old—tower over the heart of the swamp. Though related to pine and cedar, baldcypresses drop their needles, standing "bald" during the winter. Stripped of their verdant leaves, the smooth gray trunks resemble Doric columns. They support a canopy of twining vines and branches that filters the sunlight, hushes the breezes, even seems to quiet the footsteps of visitors.

Fallen giants, decaying baldcypress trunks now half submerged in black water, are nurseries for strap ferns and wild Boston ferns. A practiced eye can spot snakes, five-lined skinks, and even young alligators sunning between the lacy clumps. Amid the lush still life, a statuesque green-backed heron waits for minnows to stray from the cover of wrinkled water lettuce leaves.

This particular dry season about 400 pairs of wood storks are nesting in the lofty baldcypresses on the far side of Lettuce Lake. Recently added to the endangered species list, wood storks here are declining so rapidly that, at the present rate, the population at Corkscrew will disappear shortly after the turn of the century.

Stork expert M. Philip Kahl says they are decreasing because too many southeastern wetlands have been drained. In some years wood storks can't find enough food to raise their chicks. Corkscrew Swamp is one of the few successful rookeries left in southern Florida. Kahl calls it the "most critical U.S. breeding ground for American wood storks."

Wood storks are triggered to begin breeding when con-

centrations of fish begin increasing in swamp waterholes. By January or February in a normal winter dry season, small fish are trapped in dwindling pools. Kahl describes conditions in the ponds as "fish soup."

"I've reached my own hand in," Kahl relates, "and caught as many as 100 fish. Storks feed by touch, and in order to feed efficiently, they need high densities."

Wood stork mealtime strategy is simple: land in shallow water, bend over, open beak. When a fish bumps into a stork's bill, the bill snaps shut in an amazing 1/40th of a second. Should the angling be a little slow, storks stir the water with their bright pink feet. If that's not enough to scare minnows into their gaping mouths, they flick open their wide wings after each step, herding fish in the proper direction.

When the water level is down, wood storks are up—nesting in the baldcypresses, that is *(above)*. Lowered water levels make it easier for the storks to find food for their ever-hungry chicks. Barred owls *(left)* glide through Corkscrew at night, hooting eerily as they roam.

CORKSCREW SWAMP SANCTUARY

A dozen or more pairs of expectant storks may share a single baldcypress. They jostle for prime nest sites, clattering their beaks and jousting in mock battle. The gangling males break sticks from nearby trees or steal from neighboring nests, then present the twigs to be arranged by their mates. Couples preen each other as they take turns incubating eggs.

After the chicks hatch, one parent remains to guard them while the other spirals upward on warm air currents. Storks may rise 2,000 feet or more, soaring as far as 60 miles in search of food. Adults gorge on fish, then return to the nest and regurgitate them for the young. A pair of storks consumes about 3.5 pounds of fish a day in order to raise two chicks.

At midday, naturalist Paul Hinchcliff guides a dozen visitors to a spot along the boardwalk near the stork rookery. "Around the turn of the century," he explains, "Corkscrew often produced 7,000 to 10,000 storks a year, though there was still great fluctuation from year to year. Now there are only enough fish in the sanctuary to support a few families. The rest must hunt elsewhere. If you remember the long drive out here, there aren't many places left where storks can feed. Housing developments, citrus groves, and pastures are replacing swamps and marshes.

"Wood storks are barometers," Hinchcliff says philosophically. Their numbers and behavior are easy to measure, compared to rails, frogs, and other small swamp creatures. He pauses as a stork sails overhead, wind whooshing across its wings. "I hope that someday you can return with your children," Hinchcliff continues, looking at two teenagers in the group, "and wood storks will still be nesting here."

Baritone grunts of a pig frog and the buzzing choruses of a thousand unseen insects fill the air. After a day of stork-watching, I retrace my steps along the boardwalk as dusk begins to fall. Half a dozen white ibises, silhouetted against a glowing orange sky, wing their way to roost in a distant clump of baldcypresses.

Anhingas and herons that fished in shallow lakes this morning are now dozing on favorite perches, but I sense a movement a few yards ahead. A tawny bobcat is sauntering down the boardwalk toward me. For a moment I am frozen, caught in its curious gaze. Then the cat turns and trots away, glancing over its shoulder before it bounds into the swamp.

By twilight the pair of barred owls is together, now wide awake and ready to hunt. *Whooall,* one hoots. Day fades into night, and the creatures of Corkscrew again have the swamp to themselves.

An early riser at Corkscrew may smell the flowers of fragrant white water lilies, which usually open only from early morning until noon *(left)*. The swamp is a breeding ground for pesky insects such as mosquitoes, but other residents help keep them in check. Baby alligators *(below),* green treefrogs and damselflies *(bottom)* all prey on insects.

Senior citizens in sneakers and sun hats emerge from their vans, binoculars in hand. Just next to them, nattily dressed Mercedes owners socialize over wine and hors d'oeuvres. It is an unusual mix—vacationing birders sharing spotting scopes with the country club set on this resort island. They wait together for the evening spectacle on Sanibel Island: the arrival of the roseate spoonbills at Ding Darling National Wildlife Refuge.

Announced by spectators' disbelieving gasps, the first spoonbills glide across the sky in a lazy V-formation. Rays of the sunset transform their wings into flaming pink translucence. Each bird, as it crosses the setting sun, glows in an electrifying moment of beauty.

The birds settle onto the mud flats and are soon joined by several more small flocks. They all begin to feed immediately, rhythmically sweeping spatulate bills back and forth through the shallow water. For the spoonbills, it is another evening of gulping down shrimp, minnows, and tasty little crabs. For the observers, it is an unforgettable sight.

Pink curlew, as old-timers called the spoonbills, appear at the end of February and remain until late summer. One of the most enjoyable ways to end a day at the refuge is to watch them from the observation tower on the auto trail. There, one may also catch a glimpse of a peregrine falcon diving on ducks in a nearby bay or a bald eagle cruising over the mangroves.

The five-mile auto trail winds across a system of dikes, with tea-colored tidal flats on the right. White ibis, stately great egrets, and fiesty herons visit these shimmering inlets to dine on an aquatic buffet. At low tide, coon oysters hang from the exposed roots of red mangrove trees, and fiddler crabs dart into their holes to escape prowling night herons.

From December through February, hundreds of pintail, blue-winged teal, and American wigeon crowd freshwater ponds on the opposite side of the loop drive. Hungry brown pelicans scoop fish into their pouches, while armadas of red-breasted mergansers sail in their midst. To an artist, the refuge is a palette of shapes, colors, and motion—mullet jumping, ospreys swooping, waterfowl gabbling, spoonbills swaying to and fro.

That's exactly what Pulitzer Prize winning cartoonist J.N. "Ding" Darling had in mind half a century ago when he reminded developers, "Ducks can't lay eggs on a picket fence." Were he alive today, the founder of the National Wildlife Federation would take pride in the dazzling collage of wildlife inhabiting the 5,000-acre refuge that bears his name.

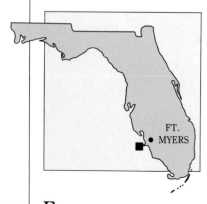

FT.
MYERS

A favorite of visitors, roseate spoonbills *(below)* return to Darling's mud flats each evening at sunset. Canoeing through this refuge *(left)* lets visitors observe its wildlife up close.

Florida's Ding Darling refuge shelters nearly 300 species of birds. Among them are the snowy egret *(left)* and the eye-catching roseate spoonbill *(right)*. Both species have rebounded after their near extinction at the hands of plume seekers in the early 1900s.

Brown pelican chicks *(far left)* may lack the appeal of some other birds, but they do demonstrate that Merritt Island is a valuable asset to wildlife. Brown pelicans have nested successfully here *(left)* and have been used to repopulate areas where pelicans were wiped out by DDT and loss of habitat. Manatees *(below)* have not fared so well. These thousand-pound mammals are endangered throughout the United States.

The blue skies over a sunny island in Mosquito Lagoon bustle with arrivals and departures of gossamer-winged herons. Birds spiral to graceful landings on whitewashed branches in the busy rookery. Bleating chicks beg to be fed. Restless hatchlings lurch to the edges of their flimsy nests, flapping quill-stubbled wings and practicing for the day they too will soar over the shallow estuary.

Meanwhile, sleek jets circle high above the birds, and on the southern horizon, engineers prepare another shuttle to explore the realms of space.

Rockets and wildlife—a curious combination. In the 1960s and '70s, dozens of rockets a year were launched here. As NASA expanded, it bought this land as a 140,000-acre buffer around Cape Canaveral on Florida's east coast. (Besides, errant rockets make lousy neighbors.) Kennedy Space Center occupies the central tract. The surrounding beach, wetland, and pine forest are managed by Merritt Island National Wildlife Refuge and Canaveral National Seashore. It is a surprisingly pleasant association. The area shelters more threatened and endangered species than any other refuge on this continent. Some smoke and noise at launch time may send clouds of birds fluttering, but otherwise the wildlife seems undisturbed.

One of the most lovable residents around Merritt Island is the easygoing manatee. Attracted to Mosquito Lagoon and Indian River by lush beds of aquatic grasses, the walrus-shaped, 1,000-pound mammals spend up to a third of their time eating, and the rest, resting. Each consumes up to 100 pounds of plants a day. Using paddle-shaped flippers, manatees literally shovel food into their mouths.

An encounter with a manatee typically begins as a gray shadow in the water beside your boat. Pause, and you'll hear a quick rush of air as the manatee surfaces to breathe. Curiosity aroused, it may gaze at you with its tiny, deep-set eyes before diving again. Sailors of yore (who must have been at sea a long time) named the animals "sirens" for their resemblance to mermaids. "Sea cow" seems more fitting in light of their voracious appetites and elephantine waistlines.

Manatees aren't the only creatures on the refuge who chow down. Along the six-mile Black Point Trail, a popular auto tour, you'll see anhingas spearing, long-necked egrets stabbing, and wood storks groping for various kinds of fish.

A brown pelican, intent on catching a mullet, breaks into a quick roll and dives headlong into the blue-green water. In a few seconds it bobs to the surface, pouch bulging. As the bird shoves its beak into the air, water dribbles out both sides, and the outline of a wriggling fish appears in its shrinking gullet. In one motion, the pelican gulps the fish and springs into flight.

The feeding pelicans are a joy to watch, and, from a boat, with binoculars you can see the hideaways among the mangroves where the birds nest. Pelican nests are homey piles of twigs and marsh grass, decorated with feathers. Parents incubate two or three creamy white eggs, which in a month hatch into naked brown chicks. Usually one sibling outcompetes its nestmates, begging for predigested fish that the parents regurgitate into their pouches. Weaker chicks fall victim to predatory gulls, ghost crabs, and crows. Still, more than 800 pairs of pelicans nested here successfully in 1988.

Along portions of the drive, vistas have changed little since explorers discovered Florida five centuries ago. To those adventurers, who arrived in wooden ships, the word "flight" meant the lilting motion that keeps flocks of gulls aloft over the surf. Along the same road today, one's thoughts turn to flight of a different kind—thundering spaceships that carry human dreams aloft to the moon and stars. The wonder of this place is that rockets and wildlife coexist in such harmony.

Before dawn on February 7, 1812, violent tremors heaved the earth along the Mississippi River in western Tennessee. Boat captains reported that trees toppled, bottomlands sank, and the river boiled like a muddy caldron. For hours the Mississippi flowed backward, filling swampy Bayou de Chien and creating Reelfoot, an elongated lake that can cover 15,000 acres when full.

Despite its tumultuous birth in this earthquake, Reelfoot Lake is now the centerpiece of a placid wildlife refuge and adjoining state park. "This shallow water is some of the best waterfowl habitat in the world," vows Reelfoot's assistant manager, Glenn Stanley. Each spring hundreds of great blue herons and great egrets nest in stately cypress trees on the lake's west side. Gadwalls, wigeons, and mallards crowd the refuge in the fall, and up to 100,000 Canada geese visit to escape severe northern winters.

The real cool-weather celebrities, however, are bald eagles. Almost 300 have been recorded here in a winter. Few sights are more thrilling than a mature bald eagle soaring overhead, white pate and tail glistening against the crisp blue sky. When it spots prey, the eagle pirouettes into the wind, skims inches above the chilly water, and plunges in with both feet to grab lunch. Powerful wingbeats carry it aloft again to perch and dine, regal in its splendor.

In winter, naturalists from the adjoining state park lead popular bald eagle tours. They begin on Upper Blue Bayou, where birders usually spot a few of the stocky birds resting in the cypresses. Then tours move to one of the eagles' favorite fishing spots on the south side of Reelfoot Lake.

Reelfoot's eagles build aeries along the upper Mississippi River, but recently a few eagles have nested at the refuge. Stanley attributes this to a project in which eight-week-old eaglets from other states are placed in artificial nests and raised at Reelfoot. Reelfoot has fledged 43 eagles since 1981.

Locals claim Reelfoot Lake is one of the world's most prolific natural fish hatcheries. Pugnacious crappies and bass lurk around the shoreline, which is still lined with the stumps of trees flooded when the lake was created. Now and then a swirl of brown water roils amid the stumps. A bowfin in search of food has stirred the mud. But considering the lake's position atop an active faultline, it's easy to wonder if another tremor is underway. Deep below, the earth does still shift. Geologists say that in the next 50 years, there is a 90 percent probability an earthquake will rock the zone in which Reelfoot lies, and the land along the Mississippi will heave and slide again.

NASHVILLE

Anglers at Reelfoot Lake *(left)* sometimes compete with great blue herons *(far left)* to catch some of the more than 50 species of fish. Created by a violent earthquake in 1812, Reelfoot today is a tranquil haven for about 300 endangered bald eagles *(below)*.

The September sun sizzles across Okefenokee National Wildlife Refuge in southeastern Georgia. Black skin glistening with steam, a 200-pound alligator hauls herself from the shallow water and scoots into the shade of some titi shrubs. She rests her head near a bulging pile of mud and rotting grasses.

Umph . . . umph, umph. A series of soft grunts emanates from deep within the conical mound. The gator slides forward, pausing at the top of the heap to listen intently. Then she digs into the pile, shoveling plant stems and soil aside with alternating strokes of her front feet. Within minutes the gator strips away a 10-inch layer of muck, revealing a cache of her eggs. Several of her lithe babies have already hatched and they slither past her, tumbling into the water.

One of the leathery spheres rolls to a stop at the edge of the nest. The shell ripples, then a tiny black head pops through. The baby gator blinks and wiggles free from its chalky prison. *Umph,* it grunts. *Umph, umph* reply the little ones already in the water. The hatchling wanders off in their direction. Meanwhile, the mother, sensing the time for birth is near, has mouthed another unhatched egg, backed down her muddy path to the water, and chomped repeatedly on the shell to free the young gator. She opens her jaws and a baby swims free from her toothy grin.

Okefenokee. Mere mention of the name conjures images of a world where alligators and snakes outnumber human visitors. The 25-by-38-mile swamp remains one of the nation's wildest wetlands.

In the 1820s, Seminole Indians hid here to escape life on a reservation. Eventually they retreated to the Everglades. Seminoles were replaced by swampers, self-sufficient men who supplemented their farm income with traplines and moonshine stills. The baldcypress harvest of the early 1900s came closest to changing the swamp forever. After removing more than a billion board feet of timber, the loggers departed. Rusting boilers and broken machinery left behind on Billy's Island are today nearly obliterated by second growth loblolly and slash pine, testament to nature's recuperative powers.

Visitors can see the edges of the swamp from the visitor center parking lot, but the watery world of the Okefenokee is best explored by canoe. Enter from the east along the Suwanee Canal, and vast watery prairies dominate the view. At Okefenokee Swamp Park on the north or at Stephen C. Foster State Park on the west, vaulted cypress forests brood over blackwater sloughs. In all, 80 miles of canoe trails wind

SAVANNAH

Canoeing is the logical way to get around in Okefenokee, where seemingly stable land often moves underfoot. A raccoon *(far left)*, perhaps stuffed with turtle eggs, reclines against a pine tree while a vigilant female alligator guards her nest mound *(below)*.

Hooded pitcher plants *(below)* are so named because they have a "hood" that keeps their bases from filling with water when it rains. A prothonotary warbler has found a cozy moss-covered niche for its nest in a hollow baldcypress knee *(left)*.
Next page: A gator's-eye view reveals how Okefenokee looks between March and November, when the waterlilies bloom.

through the swamp. To spend the night, you must apply well in advance for a permit.

After a full day of canoeing, even a 20- x 30-foot pine platform looks like a deluxe campsite. These spartan rest stops, built only two feet above the swamp, are high enough to be safe from marauding animals but close enough to guarantee exciting dreams.

Before bedding down, I counted a dozen different kinds of hoots and grunts reverberating through the damp night air. A scan with a flashlight—meant to be reassuring—revealed instead the eerie green glow of scores of eyes peering at me from the surrounding shrubs. "Probably frogs," I told myself. Just past midnight, I awakened to the screams of a heron caught in an alligator's death grip.

The cheerful words of Harry Johnson, boat concessioner at the Suwanee Canal entrance, flashed through my mind. "We haven't lost anyone yet," he said as I paddled off this morning. "No one that we know of, that is."

Canoeing through the cypress is like visiting a hall of mirrors. In this topsy-turvy world, blue sky melts into blue water with swollen trunks offering the only hint where the real tree ends and the surreal reflection begins. It's not unusual to squint skyward and discover a pudgy raccoon sleeping off a big meal of crayfish on a branch draped with Spanish moss. There's a noisy pileated woodpecker around every bend, hammering into a cypress trunk in search of ants and grubs.

Cypress knees, knobby protuberances that rise from the root system, are a curiosity. They may help aerate underwater roots or support trees in shallow, slippery soil, but no one knows for sure. It is certain they make fine basking posts for cottonmouth moccasins and an array of harmless water snakes. Occasionally a bright prothonotary warbler uses a knee as a woody perch for its nest.

Weary paddlers are sometimes tempted to step out of the canoe onto what seems to be solid ground. Instead of getting a firm footing, they stagger and sway as though walking across a water bed.

The Indian translation for Okefenokee roughly means "land of trembling earth." Gases produced by decomposing plants buoy layers of peat, called blowups, to the surface, where grass and shrub roots bind the floating mats together. On windy days these islets, which appear deceptively solid, sail across the swamp, carrying chorus frogs and dragonflies along for the ride.

With so little soil to supply nutrients, several plants employ a startling tactic to survive—they eat insects. Low-growing sundew traps bugs in sweet, sticky liquid on its spoon-shaped leaves. Pitcher plant leaves are hollow, with honey-like secretions inside. Downward-pointing hairs and slippery sides direct prey to a death pit at the plant's base. Bladderwort sucks in minute aquatic creatures as they float in the placid water.

Many a canoeist has drifted ashore to inspect a bladderwort or a delicate water lotus, only to be greeted instead by a well-camouflaged gator catapulting into the water with a splash. Equally alarmed, both human and gator usually race to see who can get farthest away first.

Whirligig beetles twirl between golden-club leaves as the human interloper's heart rate returns to normal. Submerged now, but not far away, the gator blinks curiously. In the distance, a pair of sandhill cranes warble their lilting call.

As if to answer, and to renew its mastery of the swamp, the gator swells with air and arches its tail out of the water. It emits a low, rumbling bellow—a sound so powerful that water droplets dance around its vibrating throat. It is a primal beast in a primal swamp, a timeless scene typical of the Okefenokee.

Sun and sand and sea oats cast a warm invitation to visit Pea Island almost any time of year *(right)*. Fall and spring are the best seasons for viewing the migrating snow geese *(left)* that descend on this string of barrier islands off North Carolina.

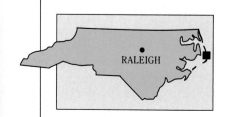

A long the North Carolina seashore, the signs of changing seasons are subtle—golden hues of sea oats instead of the northeast's dramatic autumn leaves. "Here," says Cape Hatteras ranger Connie Backlund, "we gauge the seasonal changes by arrivals and departures of the birds."

Indeed, by November, when shops selling beach balls and suntan lotion are boarded up and summer lines of traffic are distant memories, avian visitors to the Outer Banks increase dramatically. The Outer Banks—low white dunes surrounded by endless blue water—are a tenuous string of barrier islands that separate the turbulent Atlantic Ocean from placid backwaters of the North Carolina coast. Ferries and a sinewy highway transport visitors to Cape Hatteras National Seashore and Pea Island National Wildlife Refuge, which lie in the midst of this zone of crashing surf and broad horizons. Some of the sandy isles are so narrow that from the middle of the highway a traveler can see water on both sides.

To flocks of snow geese and tundra swans ending their 4,000-mile flight from the Arctic, the North Carolina coast must be a pleasant sight. So eager are these majestic birds to

The tiny piping plover incubating her speckled egg *(right)* and the ghost crab *(bottom)* live precariously on the Outer Banks, a buffer between the mainland and the ocean. Storms can dissolve shorelines or create new land overnight, sending animals scuttling for safety. Yet morning usually finds the beaches dotted with hopeful anglers *(far right)*.

reach the coast, they may have flown nonstop for the past several hours. Now they glide, necks outstretched, dark eyes searching for a safe place to land in the salt marsh ponds behind the sand dunes.

Thousands of wintering greater snow geese and good numbers of tundra swans frequent the Outer Banks. They are sometimes so thick on ponds at Pea Island that from a distance they resemble drifts of snow.

The geese awaken before sunrise, conversing in loud cackles. There is a momentary hush, then a mighty whir as countless black-tipped wings fan the air. They rise above the dunes on a steady ocean breeze. "I am here," a leader honks, "follow me." Chevrons cross, rejoin, and close ranks as the geese set a course for nearby salt meadows, where they will grub for cordgrass roots.

The stately swans ply scattered pools of deeper water, dipping their elegant heads and necks under water, emerging with black beaks full of succulent sea grasses.

Warming breezes in March find the geese and swans winging north, back to the Arctic. As they leave, other migrants reach Cape Hatteras. In the wind-pruned woodlands of Buxton and Nags Head, bright flashes of orange amid gnarled live oak branches announce the arrival of American redstarts. Bobolinks, returning from Argentina, perch on waving sea oat stalks and repeat a bubbling song that captures spring's upbeat mood in a five-second melody.

A few yards offshore, chattering flocks of gulls and terns reveal that the bluefish migration is underway. Huge schools of these fiesty predators stream north each spring, feeding on smaller fish and minnows. Fishermen, thigh-deep in the surf, cast for these prized bluefish. Many of their bites are just that; the toothy bluefish will strike at anything, including hip waders and bare legs.

By early summer, gulls, terns, and a few pelicans claim sandy banks near Pea and Bodie Islands. Piping plovers, tiny shorebirds recently added to the list of threatened species, lay their speckled eggs on flats behind the wider beaches. The eggs hatch in 28 days, and within hours of their birth, precocious chicks are pattering along behind their parents.

The cool summer sea beckons hordes of swimmers and sunbathers. As colorful coquina clams and ghostly white mole crabs tumble in the swash, children delight in catching them. Beachcombers share the shore with numerous ghost crabs, sand-colored crustaceans that peek from underground burrows. Sit quietly near one and the crab may emerge cautiously to investigate. Ghost crabs scavenge fish and other marine creatures washed in with the tide.

Short-legged sanderlings are a familiar sight, scuttling ahead of the lapping surf in search of marine worms and mollusks dislodged by the waves. Although some shorebirds summer on the Outer Banks, their numbers swell in August when migrant sandpipers, plovers, and dowitchers return from northern nesting grounds.

To islanders, the influx of shorebirds is a prelude to a mellow autumn, when kestrels, sharp-shinned hawks, and peregrine falcons soar through the sky. Northern harriers glide across the swales, flushing rice rats and voles from their grassy dens. On Bodie Island, foxes sniff at rabbit tracks in the yaupon thickets; and all along the barrier islands, monarch butterflies linger at aster and goldenrod blossoms. Thousands of these fragile orange-and-black creatures will flutter along here on their way to Mexico for the winter.

By late fall, dark strings of cormorants follow the coast south from Pea Island each morning. They fish in the chilly ocean with loons and scoters during the day, returning to shore in long beak-to-tail processions at dusk. All but the hardiest human fishermen and birdwatchers are gone now, as raw northeasters penetrate down vests and wool mittens, rattle spotting scopes, and set teeth a-chatter.

The blustery weather announces that the seasons have come full circle, and snowy wings again fill the sky. Wavering white flight lines skim overhead, close enough that you can see each bird eyeballing the shore. Snow geese and tundra swans settle once more onto the salt meadows and ponds of the Outer Banks. Their calls echo across the dunes and through the marshes. "We are here," the travelers seem to say. "We are home."

From high above, where the bald eagle soars, the view is one of bluewater bays twining through fields of waving cordgrass. Copses of darker green oaks and cedars cling to hummocks scattered throughout the surrounding marsh. This is the Lowcountry, a smorgasbord of meandering creeks, bottomland swamps, and pine-dappled ridges stretched along 35 miles of South Carolina coastline.

From Cape Romain National Wildlife Refuge on the south end to state-run Santee Coastal Reserve and the Nature Conservancy's Washo Reserve on the north, this chain of barrier islands, marshes, and swamps is a secluded slice of wild America. Together these sanctuaries provide sea turtles, pelicans, wading birds, and terns with some of their most important Atlantic nesting grounds.

Cape Island, a wave-swept spit of sand, hooks into the sea on the northeastern edge of Cape Romain refuge. Countless generations of loggerhead sea turtles have come ashore here, the only solid ground they have ever known.

At about age 20, adult females instinctively return to lay eggs on the beach where they were born. Pregnant females gather offshore in mid-May, passing the time diving for crabs, mussels, and marine snails. Loggerheads—the name refers to the massive size of the head in proportion to the body—crush these tasty morsels in their viselike jaws.

Finally, on an evening when an exceptionally high spring tide will carry them far up the beach, the females head ashore on the first of several summer egg-laying missions. Crawling ashore is no easy task for a seagoing behemoth that weighs 300 pounds. Loggerheads have streamlined flippers for efficient swimming, but without the ocean's buoyancy, the turtles flail about in the sand under the weight of their bony shells. The trail they leave in the sand resembles the workings of a small bulldozer.

Once a female reaches the dunes, she uses her rear flippers to shovel out a hole about 18 inches deep. Sticky tears pour from her eyes as she works. The watery secretions rid her body of excess salt and keep her eyes from being scratched by the shower of sand she creates. When her flippers no longer touch the bottom of the hole, the loggerhead begins to deposit scores of round, white eggs the size of Ping-Pong balls. Under the midnight moon, she heaves and sighs as they drop one by one into the nest.

Her task nearly complete, the mother turtle now fills the hole and tamps the sand. To protect the nest from predatory raccoons—who may at that very moment be gobbling eggs in

COLUMBIA

Sandy islands along the South Carolina coast provide crucial nesting sites for the endangered loggerhead sea turtle *(below)*, which can weigh up to 300 pounds. Wildlife managers try to protect these sandy beaches—hatcheries for generations of two-inch-long baby loggerheads *(left)*—from erosion and marauding raccoons that eat the newly laid eggs.

A brown pelican's bill can hold up to three times the capacity of its stomach. The pelican thus has a handy food supply ready and waiting *(right)*. Turnstones, godwits, knots, dowitchers, and orange-billed oystercatchers *(below)* can't afford such leisure, and patrol the shore for morsels they can dig up or pry open.

another nest nearby—the loggerhead instinctively tosses sand to and fro as she circles the site to disguise the nursery. About an hour after emerging from the surf, the exhausted turtle trudges back to the sea.

"Left on their own, the chances of baby turtles reaching adulthood are about 1 in 10,000," explains Larry Davis, Cape Romain's outdoor recreation planner. To help the turtles, officially listed as a threatened species, the refuge staff oversees one of the world's largest loggerhead nesting programs. "We're losing shoreline on Cape Island, where most of our turtle nesting occurs, to erosion," Davis explains. Raccoons also destroy unprotected nests.

Brilliant sunlight dances on the waves as refuge workers begin their daily patrol of the Cape Island beach. Only a few hours ago, female turtles dug here in shadowy stillness. "Fresh tracks are easy to recognize," explains refuge manager George Garris, a veteran of 10 seasons of nest relocations. "We dig up the new nests and move the eggs to higher sites, where we enclose them in mesh fencing to keep the raccoons out." Hatcheries are designed so that most of the babies can crawl out on their own when they are ready.

The warmth of the sun on the sand incubates the eggs, which hatch in two months. Baby turtles rest underground for a few more days, absorbing nourishment from their yolk sacs. Their tiny coiled shells, released from the confines of the egg, straighten and harden. At some unknown signal, the infants scramble out of the nest together, as the sand shifts between and beneath the wiggling babies, carrying them upward. The hatchlings usually surface at night. They immediately scuttle across the beach and into the water. Other than these few moments it takes to escape from the nest, male loggerheads spend their entire lives at sea.

Wind-swept Cape Island is also home to black skimmers, tern-sized birds that feed by flying low over the water, skimming fish with scissorlike beaks. They settle on the dunes, where temperatures reach 115° F on the unshaded sand, and scrape hollow depressions to deposit four speckled eggs. So perfectly do the eggs match the patterns and color of the sand, they are nearly invisible when parents leave the nest.

By contrast, the tern rookery on Marsh Island in vast Bull Bay is visible from afar. Terns are everywhere—flying in dizzying overhead formations, plunging into the water for fish, parading about at the tideline with silvery minnows to offer prospective mates. At the peak of the summer season, nearly 5,000 royal and sandwich terns squeeze their nests onto the

Carnivorous pitcher plants such as these in the marshy area of Santee Reserve trap insects to get nutrients that are lacking in the wet, sandy soil.

sandy isle. Each broods a single egg, sometimes two, in a scrape located only a wingtip away from its neighbor.

Seen from a boat just off shore, the tightly packed colony appears to be a restless sea of white heads and stark black crests. Deafening tern chatter blends with the raucous voices of the 1,500 laughing gulls that nest nearby. The din drifts downwind, along with the acrid odor of guano and dead fish.

Terns and skimmers fish in the waters surrounding Bulls Island, the centerpiece of Cape Romain National Wildlife Refuge. The pine-studded island supports a sizeable population of alligators in its shallow pools and a variety of water birds, including pelicans, swans, and wood storks, in its marshes.

Accessible by boat from the refuge dock, Bulls Island is only 6.5 miles long by 2 miles at its widest point, but offers hiking trails that traverse thick maritime forests, circle cattail-fringed ponds, and spill onto a desolate, windswept beach. On some days, your own footprints may be the only sign of human activity among the storm-tossed sand dollars and barnacle-encrusted whelk shells.

Davis, an energetic man who spends quite a bit of time afield, advises, "Spring is a good time to visit. Early in the season, mosquitoes aren't a problem, and on warm days the big alligators will be out sunning. You'll see brown pelicans and lots of shorebirds along the front beach." About 2,500 pelican nests were noted on Marsh Island at Cape Romain in 1988.

Gators rarely threaten visitors, but a few may hiss when defending babies or a prized sunning spot. It's best to come no closer than 30 feet.

The three-mile trail through Washo Reserve is another excellent place to encounter wildlife. In the shadowy stillness, flat-shelled turtles, "cootuhs" in the local parlance, blink as sunbeams filter down through the towering cypress trees. High above, a great blue heron patiently sits on a bulging stick nest. Snowy egrets roost among the tupelo branches at half that height. One of the immaculate white birds checks the pale green eggs beneath its breast, then settles back, shaking its trailing plumes like a nervous bride rearranging her veil. Hatchling survival is high, thanks to guardian alligators that patrol the duckweed-covered water. They intercept marauding raccoons before they can climb the trees to steal the eggs.

Washo Reserve, a cypress-tupelo bottom, was dammed in the 1700s to provide water for a rice plantation. The backwater has been an important rookery for nearly two centuries. After the surrounding rice fields were abandoned, beavers, frolicking otters, deer, wild turkeys, and wood ducks proliferated on land now included in the Santee Coastal Reserve.

The halcyon days of summer in the Lowcountry end with the first chilly blow from the northwest. White-capped waves froth across Bull Bay, sending sea turtles and terns searching for warmer climes. Teal appear on the horizon, distant specks against the low, scudding clouds.

By October, pintails, shovelers, and wigeons settle in to winter on the wide Santee River delta. When snow finally blankets the North, black ducks, jaunty mallards, ruddy ducks, canvasbacks, and scaup arrive en masse. In good years, more than 150,000 migrants wade and dive within the Romain and Santee preserves.

Twice a day, as the tide ebbs from the marshes, muddy clumps of oysters are exposed. American oystercatchers, known locally as "oyster crackers," stroll through the muck, thrusting their orange stiletto beaks into the bivalves and savoring each tasty prize.

Nearby, a sun-bleached raccoon also patters through the mud, sampling clams and nosing along behind a retreating army of fiddler crabs. Long before the raccoon's curiosity is satisfied, the rising tide drives it back to shore.

From high above, the eagle sees creeks swollen once more with the rich tidal flow. Water imparts a sense of balance to the Lowcountry—sloughs winding through stately cypress swamps, rivulets trickling amid the cordgrass, the dynamic interface of waves and sand. Here, where land and sea meet so harmoniously, lie some of the most bountiful wildlife sanctuaries on the entire Atlantic shore.

F allout! The news flashes across bird-alert hotlines, and eager birdwatchers depart for the coast of Louisiana. They want to see, as in the tale of Chicken Little, a sky that is falling—literally raining birds. Larry McNease, a biologist at Louisiana's Rockefeller Refuge, calls the fallout "a phenomenal experience."

The saga begins 600 miles south when migrant songbirds leave Central America. They follow a straight-line course over the Gulf of Mexico, normally an 18-hour flight. But when spring cold fronts collide with moist ocean air, chilly thunderstorms can leave the rain-soaked vagabonds struggling across the sea. Energy reserves depleted, they finally come to rest in a string of wildlife refuges along the Louisiana coast.

After storms like this, the slender saltbush boughs at Rockefeller and Sabine National Wildlife Refuge can drip with exhausted rose-breasted grosbeaks, scarlet tanagers, and indigo buntings. Each shrub rivals a breathtaking Christmas tree, adorned with living ornaments. No wonder birders flock to the scene, where they can sometimes observe three colorful species in the same binocular view.

The tiny travelers lose about 30 percent of their weight during the flight. Still far from their nest sites in the north, they refuel on seeds, berries, mosquitoes, and calorie-rich caterpillars. Some birds will depart at nightfall. Others remain a few days in this land of bayous and cheniers. The cheniers, sandy ridges with the first trees the birds have encountered since the Yucatan, are vital rest stops on the birds' journey.

Inland, fall flocks of pintail ducks and snow geese land among the water lilies at Lacassine refuge. About 300,000 waterfowl dabble in the refuge's ponds and potholes. "This is the best place in the world to see white-fronted geese," says Paul Yakupzack, Lacassine's assistant manager.

Even when fallouts don't occur and the ducks and geese are not migrating, these marshes are seldom empty. Nutria paddle through the marsh waters, browsing on vegetation or returning to stream-bank burrows to mate and reproduce. An introduced species, the prolific nutria are valuable for their fur, and only continued harvesting by the fur industry prevents nutria numbers from reaching damaging levels.

Spring belongs to shimmering spoonbills that nest on Rabbit Island, east of Sabine. Hundreds of swamp rabbits scamper about in summer. Add some alligators basking on mudbanks and blue crabs scuttling in the shallow bayous, and you have a wildlife mix as rich as any Creole gumbo. Sampling it, at any season, can be a delectable experience.

BATON ROUGE •

The rose-breasted grosbeak *(far left)* is one of many species of songbird that pass through Louisiana on their way north in the spring. Farmers welcome this colorful bird because it eats potato beetles and the seeds of many weeds. Four-day-old swamp rabbits *(below)* win points on looks alone.

Southern Louisiana is astir with pudgy nutria *(left)* and the white-faced ibis *(above)*. An introduced species, nutria were once considered a pest. Their numbers have since stabilized, and they are often trapped for their fur. Ibises use their curved bills to probe for frogs, grasshoppers, and crawfish.

THE NORTHEAST

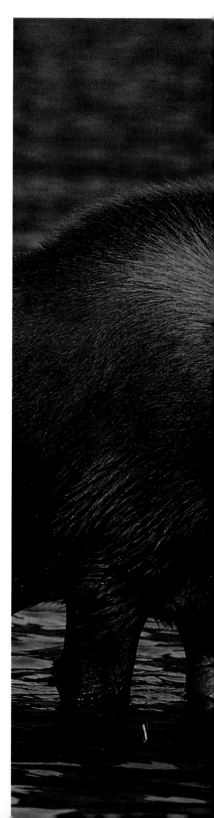

Preceding page: Veiled by clouds, Mt. Katahdin looms over Baxter State Park as a young moose pauses to investigate a distant noise.

Greg Hamer, a ranger at Baxter State Park in Maine, keeps a moose-o-meter on the wall beside his desk. Park visitors, who often come to Baxter hoping for a glimpse of these imposing and wonderfully homely animals, can move a little arrow to various wedge-shaped sections characterizing the results of their moose-watching. The wedges are labeled "Bull Moose Feeding," "Cow Moose Beauty Contest," "Moose Diving Off Big Rock," "Multiple Moose," "Moose Rutting Activity," "Cow and Calf," and "No Moose Out." The arrow seldom points to the last choice because the moose are almost always out at Baxter, perhaps the best true wilderness park in the East.

"People love to see them," Hamer says. "They come back from Sandy Stream Pond and tell me all kinds of stories—they saw a calf riding on its momma's back, two bulls fighting, anything." Hamer has been observing moose long enough that he can reproduce a credible moose mating call on a horn made from birch bark. It sounds a little like the horn of an antique Ford. "August isn't the best time to see them," he cautions, "because they get tired of people by the end of summer." But he urges us to walk a well-traveled path to the pond to find out for ourselves.

Our escort, a bright-eyed young seasonal ranger named Sandy Tardiff, puts a finger to her lips as we come in sight of the pond. A half-dozen people stand on a wooden walkway at the edge of the water. One raises two fingers in a "V" and silently points: two moose, grazing on water plants. "That's a cow and a yearling male," Tardiff whispers. "You can tell he's young because of that scrawny little rack—nubbers, we call antlers like that." The two moose are feeding about 50 yards apart in a pond in the shadow of 5,267-foot Mt. Katahdin, the park's centerpiece. The stillness is absolute except for the gentle splash of a moose snout breaking water and the irreverent squawks of passing ducks. It is a moment of such tranquility that snapping a picture seems a vulgar intrusion.

The yearling suddenly breaks the stillness in a clatter of hoofbeats. Apparently scolded by his mother, the flustered young bull charges off in ear-flapping disarray, like a chastened cocker spaniel. Ten feet from where we stand, he abruptly turns and halts, mouth agape as he gasps to catch his breath. Only then does he notice us—eyesight is not a moose strong point—but he seems too fussed to care. "That was a don't-eat-my-food move," Tardiff explains. "The kid hasn't learned the rules yet."

As we were watching, a third moose, larger than the

BANGOR

Patience brings its reward, as two delighted women at Sandy Stream Pond get an up-close view of a moose *(left)*. Baxter's shallow ponds are ideal places to spot moose, which plunge in to feed on aquatic plants containing much-needed sodium.

During breeding season, or "rut," bull moose sometimes battle each other *(below)* for the chance to mate with a cow. Bulls all but forget to eat during these few frenzied weeks, leaving the best willow twigs for hungry beavers *(right)*.

other two (bulls weigh up to 1,400 pounds), high-stepped over a rock into the pond with an oddly tentative stride and began grazing. The yearling stilled his thumping heart and presently moved off. Serenity returned.

"There's something likeable about moose," Tardiff says. "They're funny and regal-looking at the same time. They just inspire affection—mine, anyway."

A loon materialized on the pond as a thick mist settled over Katahdin, a mountain that Henry David Thoreau once described as a "cloud factory." Thoreau's account of his trip here introduced many easterners to the mountain. Katahdin and the densely forested, lake-spangled wilderness that spreads out from its flanks have changed surprisingly little since Thoreau scaled the peak in 1846. The sage of Walden Pond found the wildness of the place, its incarnation of "primeval, untamed and forever untamable nature," at once awful and beautiful. The idea of preserving the area as a wilderness park was an obsession of Percival Baxter, who served as Maine's governor during the 1920s and ramrodded the creation, in 1931, of a sanctuary that would be "forever held in its natural wild state."

Baxter Park's raw, uncompromising wildness sets it apart from other preserves in the East. Distances seem longer here and silences deeper. Fewer visitors come here (82,000 in 1987) than to other retreats like the Adirondacks. One has to work to reach Baxter's away-from-it-all site in northern Maine and one has to be prepared for it. Winter arrives in October and persists until May, and the park's search-and-rescue teams regularly trek into Baxter's back country to retrieve lost or injured climbers and cold-weather hikers suffering from frostbite. Man's intrusions have been deliberately held to a minimum: a slow, unpaved road, several campgrounds, hiking trails—but no stores or lodges, gas stations or snack bars. "And there won't be any," chief ranger Chris Drew declares. "We'll continue to manage the park as a primitive area because that's its appeal." Baxter shines as a western-quality wilderness park in the East.

Its 313 square miles are an island of evergreens and deciduous trees in the largely cut-over Maine forest. "If you look at a satellite picture you see this green rectangle with bare brown places around its edges," says Drew. "That's the park and the clear-cut patches." Baxter contains 18 peaks above 3,000 feet, mere hills by western standards but wild and intimidating nonetheless. The park boasts medicinal herbs like the purple-flowered mint known as "self-heal," said to cure

both wounds and sore throats. Wildflower fanciers can find the painted trillium, starflower, bunchberry, and other bright-hued species. The park's 178 miles of hiking trails include the final stretch of the 2,000-mile-long Appalachian Trail, which ends on one of Mt. Katahdin's burly shoulders.

The spruce, fir, and pine forests and the lakes and streams studded among the trees harbor a splendidly diverse wildlife community. Park officials estimate the moose numbers at 750, but local outdoorsmen suspect there might be more Bullwinkles than that in the park. The number of black bears has held steady at about 200 in recent years, though they are harder to see since the park closed its dumps.

In addition, Baxter State Park is home to rarely seen critters like the dark-coated fisher and the related pine marten, whose beautiful coat is commercially known as sable. Otters and energetic beavers conduct their business in the dark, rushing streams. Eastern coyotes, bulkier than their western cousins, have become so abundant that their lonely nocturnal howls now compete with the haunting cries of the loons. A visitor has to be almost criminally unlucky to spend time in Baxter without seeing a wild beast.

Moose are of course the leading crowd-pleasers. They're easy to see because of their bulk (nine feet long, seven and one half feet high at the shoulders) and their preference for known ponds and marshes. Moose are fond of boggy, shallow ponds because of the aquatic plants there, which supply needed sodium in the animals' diet. The generally placid disposition of moose makes them a favorite with visitors, too.

Indeed, the indifference moose show to humans strikes some as almost rude. Moose are solitary, nearsighted vegetarians who feed in the park's low areas during summer and move to higher country in winter. Their spasms of aggression are normally limited to the autumn rutting season. "They've treed visitors and even rangers," Drew says, "for 20 minutes at a time. If you run into one on a trail you want to give him the right of way because he's going to hold his ground."

People find moose entertaining because of their looks ("They appear to have been put together by a committee," Maine hunting guide Ron Masure once observed.), their nonchalance, and their occasional lapse into outright foolishness. "They're a little slow, and I'm being kind," Masure said. "A moose will bump into a wall, pause, then turn away." Guide Wilmot "Wiggy" Robinson, who often takes fishing parties into the area, once came upon a young moose asleep on its feet. The groggy moose barely stirred as Wiggy looped a rope

Baxter's dense woodlands, ornamented by 64 ponds and lakes, shelter a rich mixture of animals, including white-tailed deer fawns, tiger swallowtail butterflies, and red squirrels. Maine's away-from-it-all park was created in 1931 as a sanctuary that would be "forever held in its wild state."

around its neck and led the unprotesting animal down a trail.

Wildlife photographer Dwight Kuhn and a friend were waiting for moose at Sandy Stream Pond one warm afternoon when his friend dozed off. He awoke to discover a moose snout about three feet from his face, the large brown eyes studying him without rancor.

Shaggy moose stories predominate, yet Baxter's other four-legged residents can also be fascinating to encounter. Ranger Sandy Tardiff was birding by a pond when three otter heads suddenly surfaced like periscopes and took a bead on her. They climbed onto a log, eyed her curiously and then scooted off. Chris Drew provoked a hiss from a startled otter when he glided within 15 feet of it in a canoe. Tardiff was less charmed the time she was working at the park gate and the sliding door suddenly opened to a width of about three inches for no discernible reason. She looked out the window and saw a small black bear trying to paw the door open. When she spoke sternly to it, the intruder scrambled off.

The Atlantic puffin can gather several small fish at once as it torpedoes along under water. The bird's tongue pushes the fish back, then slight notches inside its upper bill keep the fish secure until the puffin can deliver them to its young.

BANGOR

From a distance the 20-acre chunk of rock in the Atlantic 10 miles off the Maine coast looks like nothing more than a menace to navigation, with a lonely lighthouse standing vigil. But on a closer look it appears that somebody's home after all—the sea birds. Gulls and terns complain noisily about the steady wind as they glide amid the wave-washed rocks on the low outcrop called Machias Seal Island. The shearwaters above them go about their business soberly and patiently. Comic relief comes from those puffins clustered on a roof near the lighthouse, nodding and waddling and flashing their tricolored bills. Puffins can't help it: they always look as if they're about to tell a joke.

Formally attired in black coats and white waistcoats, rocking from side to side in their orange-footed strut, the engaging puffins seem designed for pursuits other than flight.

"I saw one try to take off from flat ground once while it was looking the wrong way," says Captain Barna B. Norton, who carries 500 to 800 visitors to the island on his boat each summer. "It smacked into a building. I was almost ashamed to laugh. I think maybe they're not supposed to fly," the skipper adds in his downeast Maine accent. "But nobody told them that. And they nevah read it."

In flight puffins point their red-yellow-gray beaks resolutely at the ground and appear to be concentrating hard. Their colorful schnoz and somewhat jaunty manner account for the alias they sometimes go by—"sea parrots."

Though Machias Seal Island is American territory, its lighthouse is manned by the Canadian Coast Guard, and a Canadian wildlife officer spends two months there each summer. The puffins hang around slightly longer, arriving punctually in mid-April and exiting in middle to late August after producing the next generation in nests amid the rocks and grassy patches. Puffins breed in burrows that they have shoveled out in soft ground, propelling showers of earth with their strong feet. Norton estimates that 2,500 nested on the island in 1988. Scientists are especially impressed by puffin parents as providers for their young: they can bring home as many as 10 to 20 little fish in their triangular bills at a time. After about 40 days, the chick is on its own, and it soon gets ready to make its first hazardous journey to the sea. Atlantic puffins winter on the open ocean between Maine and Greenland.

The seals that gave the island its name before abandoning it to the birds have shifted their headquarters to another isle a few miles away. There's no proof of this, but they may have grown tired of the puffins' jokes.

Along the coast of Maine, arctic terns *(right)* wheel and dive. Some of these avian globe-trotters migrate from the Arctic to the Antarctic and back each year, logging in more than 22,000 miles round trip.

Atlantic puffins join the terns at rocky outcrops of land such as Machias *(below)* to nest in spring. The puffins remain in their colonies *(next page)* until mid-summer, when they return to sea and begin autumn molt.

Most of the snow geese have passed through the refuge by the end of October, but an early November sunrise reveals a few lingering sojourners. Refuges like this one make a series of steppingstones for migrating waterfowl, places for the birds to nest and refuel on a taxing journey of hundreds of miles.

ATLANTIC
CITY

The refuge was established mainly for the protection of waterfowl, but its tidal marshes also attract double-crested cormorants *(right),* red-winged blackbirds *(below),* and great blue herons *(below right).* This rich variety causes devoted birdwatchers to descend in droves every spring and fall.

The advance guard appears one day in late September, a detachment of a few dozen strong fliers, vividly white with black tips on their wings. For weeks the snow geese have been beating their way south from their arctic breeding grounds. When the forerunners drop gracefully onto the freshwater marsh on the New Jersey coast, the word immediately goes out on the birdwatchers' telegraph—they're back—and nature lovers from all over begin plotting a trip to the refuge at Brigantine, the place many of them think of as birder heaven.

Three days later 500 snow geese float serenely on the pools and saltwater inlets at the sanctuary officially known as the Edwin B. Forsythe National Wildlife Refuge, a few miles across the mud flats from the glitter and glitz of Atlantic City. Then the geese begin to arrive in great ivory swarms, settling onto the pools and marsh like some ground-hugging snow cloud. By December their numbers usually have peaked, in some years as high as 40,000, and the binoculars-wielding birders seem almost as numerous. The stars of this annual spectacle feed on Brigantine's bounty of marsh grass until the first freeze in late November or December sends them winging farther south—and the refuge seems suddenly lonely.

But not really. The dark-winged sea geese called brant are still there, cruising offshore in hordes as large as those of the snow geese, but more distant and harder to see. Diving ducks and rough-legged hawks are still around and a pair of endangered peregrine falcons, charisma champions of the avian world, has lived at the refuge during nesting season for several years. Brigantine is, in fact, a joy at any time, save possibly on a still summer morning when those unrelenting mosquitoes are abuzz.

Though white-tailed deer and other animals thrive in the woods bordering the marsh, it's the aerial show that brings nearly 200,000 people a year to Brigantine. "The refuge is one of a kind," declares manager David Beall. "It's the combination of a freshwater pool, a brackish pool, and the surrounding salt marsh that attracts a tremendous abundance and diversity of birds"—289 species at last count.

The main venue for visitors is an eight-mile-long gravel road on a dike that rings the freshwater and brackish pools, with tidal marshes and open bay on the outer side. The one-way road makes birdwatching almost sinfully easy; a car acts as a blind and the viewing is better if you stay in the car. The snow geese congregate in the freshwater pool, but they're only the most visible of the birds that return regularly to Brigantine. Green-winged teal, black ducks, and gadwall pass through in season, along with great blue herons, cormorants, osprey and several kinds of egrets. During one three-day period in September the register in which visitors record their sightings listed bitterns, a peregrine, a bald eagle, several types of hawk, four starlings (someone wrote "big deal" next to this entry), and a man named Ed, who mistakenly entered his name where the species is supposed to go.

A slow-motion drive on the loop road is a "can't-miss" wildlife-watching experience, especially soon after the refuge opens its gate at sunrise. A cormorant flicks its head from side to side and then vanishes underwater, only to resurface 30 seconds later and 20 feet away after a deep dive to catch fish. Its hunger sated, the bird awkwardly high-steps across the surface and takes off, transforming itself in flight into a black spear with a curved handle.

A great blue heron, moving with stateliness through a shallow pool, stops and crosses its toothpick legs distractedly, then unlimbers its sinuous neck to its full lethal length and with a darting move strikes its wiggly prey. A snowy egret, having lured a meal by flicking its bright yellow feet under water, struggles with a flapping fish that won't fit neatly into its beak. A northern harrier glides in lazy arcs against a backdrop of the five-mile-distant Atlantic City skyline, the buildings aligned tidily in the gray haze like hotels on a Monopoly board.

In the freshwater pool a dozen gadwall ducks feed with heads underwater and rumps tipped up as in a can-can. Gulls, whose ubiquity makes them perhaps the most ignored and maligned of water birds, are everywhere, but hardly anybody talks about them. One member of this friendless gull tribe plops into the water three feet from a marsh duck, which also ignores it. An entire gull village takes refuge from the wind —the blessed, mosquito-routing wind—in the lee of a marsh-grass island. Meanwhile three cattle egrets in search of insects stare intently at roadside grass until a car's wheels are almost on top of them, then fussily flap off to an equally perilous station a few yards ahead.

Near the end of the road a tornado-like cloud, swooping and swirling and constantly changing shape, resolves itself into a flock of chittering swallows. The black cloud whips around in another precisely choreographed circle before dropping to a grassy field in a final, sublimely orchestrated swoop. The swallows are guided by a mysterious communications system that biologists still don't fully understand, but it only adds to the wonder and delight of birdwatching at Brigantine.

Don Riepe spies the peregrine cruising maybe 500 yards over the marsh fringing Jamaica Bay. The bird is suspended momentarily above the hazy line of towers that is downtown Manhattan, but then it shifts gears and goes into a diagonal high-speed stoop aimed at a cluster of gulls idling in marsh grass. The hurtling peregrine comes within inches of one frightened gull before it veers off and a cloud of gulls flutters up in dismay. "He was just teasing," explains Riepe, a natural resources specialist. "It's pandemonium when a peregrine appears, but he was just buzzing them. It's sort of like play, but they give a peregrine the greatest respect."

It is the juxtaposition of wildlife as rare and splendid as a peregrine falcon and the gritty urbia of New York City that gives Jamaica Bay Wildlife Refuge its singular character. The 9,155-acre refuge, visited annually by about 100,000 people, is a metropolitan stress-reliever within walking distance of a subway station. It originated in a political tradeoff. When the New York City Transit Authority proposed dredging sand from Jamaica Bay for a subway embankment in the early 1950s, parks commissioner Robert Moses agreed to the plan only if the authority built two freshwater impoundments at the same time. Trees, shrubs, and grasses were planted around the ponds to attract wildlife. In 1972 the refuge became part of the National Park Service's Gateway National Recreation Area. The NPS reintroduced species such as painted turtles and spring peepers that once were abundant in the area.

The refuge that resulted is a garden of wildness and stillness amid the rush and clatter of the city. Peregrines nest on nearby bridges. Owls and sparrows lay their eggs in fields next to runways at neighboring John F. Kennedy Airport. Several kinds of geese, ducks, and wading birds forage within blocks of busy major boulevards. "People are always telling me that they find a solitude here they can't get anywhere else in the city," says Riepe.

Riepe leads us to East Pond, a freshwater lake that visitors reach by jaywalking across busy Crossbay Boulevard. Canada geese, ruddy ducks, and the sometimes ill-tempered mute swans sail serenely on the pond; egrets and night herons bivouac near shore; and butterflies flitter around the shrubs. "This is a good place to see monarchs, 'question marks' and other migrating butterflies," he says. Fifty species have been sighted here. A silver sky-whale with GOODYEAR on its side hovers over Shea Stadium a few miles away.

Riepe, who has worked at Gateway since 1979, can

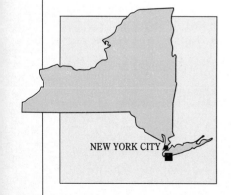

This young black-crowned night heron keeps a wary watch for predators as it settles in for a day of sunbathing and sleeping at Jamaica Bay, one of the nation's most urban wildlife refuges. These herons usually stalk their prey after sunset.

NEW YORK CITY

Wall Street's hubbub is only a
subway ride away, but Canada
geese and other wild creatures
rest serenely at Jamaica Bay
(below). Comblike "teeth" on a
male northern shoveler's broad
bill *(bottom)* help it strain plants
and tiny animals from the
refuge's marshes and ponds.

identify every plant, fish, bird, and mammal species on the
premises. "As long as you don't take me away from here I'm
okay," he cheerfully admits. "But put me in the Adirondacks
and I'm lost."

The combination of freshwater ponds and the bay in-
creases the diversity of bird life at the refuge—326 species
have been identified over the past 30 years—but the belt of
civilization that girds the preserve limits any abundance of
mammals. One exception is noticeable just after Easter each
year, when a few bunnies, illegally liberated on the refuge by
their reluctant city-bred owners, suddenly turn up.

The greens capture your eye first. Golf course green, prairie springtime green, St. Patrick's Day tie green, spearmint green, Vermont license plate green, mountain meadow green, spruce needle green—every green in the glorious spectrum of greenness seems mingled here, fusing and flashing amid the forests and fields of the slice of Virginia called Mt. Rogers National Recreation Area (NRA). Managed by the U.S. Forest Service, this skillet-handle-shaped preserve just north of the intersection of Virginia, Tennessee, and North Carolina has a luxuriant, sub-alpine look that's hard to find in the mild-mannered mountains of the eastern United States.

The terrain here is knobby and shaggy, not dramatic in the fashion of western peaks. All heights and shapes, the knobs fill the horizon in every direction. The pinched little flats and hollows amid the knobs have always been stingy farmland and help explain the region's poverty despite the lushness.

This is up-and-down country, a mountainous province capped by 5,729-foot Mt. Rogers, Virginia's highest. Because of its elevation, Mt. Rogers NRA is cooler than the rest of Virginia and supports a spruce-fir forest that is more reminiscent of Maine or a green patch of the Pacific Northwest than of southern Virginia.

Hundreds of miles of trails for hikers (including a 64-mile section of the Appalachian Trail), horseback riders, and other fans of the outdoors crisscross the NRA and the Jefferson National Forest that envelops it. Dogwood blossoms whiten the hillsides in the spring, and cascades of rhododendrons give the high meadows a purplish-pink cast in summer.

The abundant wildlife—white-tailed deer and turkeys, ruffed grouse and foxes and flying squirrels and a few bears that cherish their privacy—cluster on and around the grass-lands that mountaineers call "mountain balds": meadowlike spaces interspersed with scattered trees and rock outcrops.

The richest of the mountain balds is a 2,200-acre section accessible only on foot, on horseback, or by four-wheel-drive vehicle on a rugged road. It's called the Crest Zone because it's about a thousand feet below the rounded crest of Mt. Rogers. Because of its rich grasses and browse, in addition to its isolation, the Crest Zone attracts more kinds of wildlife than any place else in the NRA. "I don't think there's any place else in the Appalachians where there's that big a bald," says ranger Cecil Thomas, a blond-bearded North Carolinian. "The variety of plant and animal life there is tremendous."

Flighty white-tailed deer are the zone's most visible and

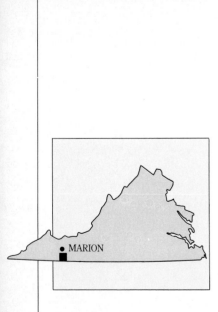

MARION

On the knobby mountain "balds" of Mt. Rogers *(below)*, rabbits *(left)* and groundhogs *(far left)* forage for food. This rocky, windswept habitat is more typical of coastal Maine than of southern Virginia.

A resourceful raccoon can scale almost anything which provides a toehold. Abundant in the Virginia mountains, they often pass the day in a tree *(left)*, napping or perhaps sniffing out which campsite to raid come nightfall.

characteristic critters. Since this habitat has everything that deer covet—plenty of browse, water, and good cover—white-tailed numbers have held steady for the past 10 years, despite regular hunting seasons and persistent poaching. Thomas, the NRA's chief of wildlife management, figures that deer average more than 20 per square mile in the Crest Zone.

Deer are of course famously spooky, and for good reason, but they're less afraid of humans on horseback than afoot, frequently permitting a mounted intruder to come within 15 feet. The deer hunker down in the shady woods bordering clearings in midday, but you may see them on the move in early morning and late afternoon. When a storm is on the way, as one often is in this country, the deer may be out eating greedily. "The weather up there is different than anywhere around it," Thomas says of Mt. Rogers, where it has been known to snow in May.

If you move with the stealth of a mountain man and get lucky to boot you might see a flock of wild turkeys or the acrobat known as the northern flying squirrel. The flying squirrel, considered endangered in Virginia, has a winglike membrane that permits it to coast downward 20 or 25 feet before landing with a gentle smack.

Turkeys, native to the Appalachians, nearly disappeared during the hard times of the 1930s when meat was where you found it, but now they're back in great gobbling hordes. While turkeys are unenthusiastic fliers (they'd rather run than fly when alarmed), they will fly when they have to. Thomas has even seen them up in the thermals—rising columns of warm air—where the hawks operate.

Somewhat slimmer than their domestic counterparts, wild turkeys nest in bushes near water and roost in trees at night. After the spring hatch they travel in flocks of several females and their half-dozen or so chicks, known as poults. Males also bunch up in flocks. Cold, damp weather is especially hard on young turkeys because they lack an effective water-repellent mechanism and thus frequently get chilled and die in spring rains.

Despite the fact that Benjamin Franklin once nominated them as our national bird, turkeys don't care much for humans. When they sense an interloper their heads jerk up, gobbling ceases, and the whole flock bustles off together like race walkers at the starting line.

Perhaps you'll be the lucky one to see the race begin as you trek the mountain balds of Mt. Rogers.

A yearling white-tailed fawn
may tag along with its mother
for another year *(left)*. Born in
mid-winter, bear cubs *(above)*
spend a year under the sow's
protection, going solo after
hibernation the next winter.

Late afternoon finds Assateague Island washed by soft light and gentle colors. The broad barrier beach, fringed by dunes greened by deep-rooted grass, sweeps down the 37-mile shoreline until its dun stripe merges with the pale blue of the late summer sky and the gray of the momentarily tranquil Atlantic. A few hundred feet inland a yellow-footed snowy egret stands at the muddy edge of a marsh, silent and motionless, while the field behind it is sprinkled with the more vivid colors of Assateague's famous ponies—chestnut and palomino and roan, brown and white, pinto and buckskin and black, every color of the equine rainbow. They nibble the stringy cordgrass that flourishes in the island's salt marshes.

But more than the colors it is the juxtaposition of sea and forest that defines Assateague. Here the sea meets the marsh, and the marsh meets the woods, and the enchantment of this island is bound up with the richness and diversity of a wildlife population blessed with a smorgasbord of habitats.

It's possible here to lose yourself in a pocket pine grove less than a mile from the beach. You can swivel your neck upward from a quiet sylvan trail and see a jumbo Delmarva squirrel, an endangered species double the size of a common gray squirrel, bustling down the straight-as-a-telephone-pole trunk of a 40-foot-high loblolly pine. Brown needles carpet the trail, warblers trill amid pines and water oaks. Both white-tailed deer and the little deerlike elk called sika, a species of elk introduced from Japan years ago, chomp the shiny leaves of greenbrier shrubs.

Assateague may hold a diversity of habitats, but in jurisdictional terms, it's a jungle. Lying on the eastern shore of Chesapeake Bay, the island is divided among two states and two Interior Department agencies. Its southern two-fifths is in Virginia and since 1943 has been a national wildlife refuge (Chincoteague) managed by the U.S. Fish and Wildlife Service. The northern part, in Maryland, has since 1965 been Assateague National Seashore, operated by the National Park Service. A barbed-wire fence curling incongruously across marsh and dunes marks the border of the two preserves.

But whatever flag it flies, Assateague is constantly changing shape, with the ocean eating away its eastern face and sand deposits lengthening its capes. The various habitats of the island support not only ponies, miniature elk, and Delmarva squirrels, but a diverse population of birds—snow geese, skimmers, ospreys, wood ducks, 307 species in all —that inspired a seventeenth-century visitor to marvel at

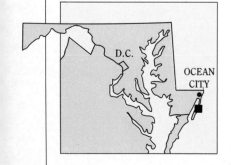

This great egret has found a perfect fishing nook in a misty Chincoteague tidal creek. From here it can easily spot the fish, frogs, and water insects that make up the bulk of its diet.

Although subspecies of sika deer are endangered in Asia, Assateague's sika *(left)* are doing just fine. Also thriving are the island's gregarious ponies. A skewbald pony *(right)* is attended by cattle egrets that feed on grasshoppers and other insects disturbed by its grazing.

later spied a flash of silver-gray on a nearby trunk. The broad swash of a tail was black-edged. It was a Delmarva squirrel, one of an estimated 2,000 that remain in the United States. The 200 at Chincoteague refuge are descendants of a colony of 32 introduced by the refuge staff two decades ago.

Some Delmarvas at Chincoteague nest in numbered boxes that refuge staffers have placed just off the Pony Trail to help monitor the numbers of squirrels. They're partial to the seeds of loblolly cones, but also feed on nuts and buds. An adult Delmarva is a heavyweight as squirrels go, weighing in at about two pounds.

A few yards farther on I saw a movement among the greenbrier leaves 10 feet off the trail. As I stared at the spot, a twitching black nose materialized in the foot-high brush. To my surprise the nose abruptly rose and a young sika, perhaps weighing all of 25 pounds, scrambled awkwardly to its feet. The fawn seemed more curious than frightened, perhaps because its mother was under a branch only a few yards away.

The sika are an exotic species that evolved in the Orient. A promoter in the nearby resort town of Ocean City, Maryland, the story goes, imported a few from Japan in the 1920s as an attraction and later donated them to the local Boy Scouts, who liberated them on Assateague. They have since multiplied to the point that both the refuge and the national seashore now permit hunting to control their numbers.

Though they look like miniature deer (an adult buck weighs about 65 pounds), the elk family resemblance is visible in the sikas' spotted backs and slanting horns and it's audible in their surprisingly full-throated bugles. "They're like loons," says refuge staffer Nancy Phelps. "They make a big sound for a small animal." Their cry, heard most often at night, sometimes sounds like a bawling human infant.

Suddenly startled, the sika fawn bounded vertically into the air with all four hooves several inches off the ground, an acrobatic feat that resulted in no forward progress. Mother and offspring then moved off through the shrubbery with a soft rustle, leaving the trail once again to two-legged critters.

The ponies celebrated in legend and literature (*Misty of Chincoteague*) are indisputably the main attraction for wildlife viewers among the million-plus people who visit Assateague annually. Stallion-led bands of 5 to 20 mares and foals graze in marshes, among dune grasses, and often along the road. Something about these horses—their short stature and sturdiness, their stunning range of colors—has always appealed to visitors. The sight of a band of pintos capering on a beach,

their "millionous multitudes." Millionous multitudes there still are. You can enjoy them from roads in both seashore and refuge, from hiking and bicycle trails and atop observation towers. You can take tours by van or stroll the woods and the edge of the marsh alone with an ear cocked for the silence.

On the September day I walked Chincoteague refuge's wooded, 1.6-mile "Pony Trail," I was less interested in ponies—I'd seen several bands already—than in the rare Delmarva fox squirrel and the delicate, collie-sized sika. Sunlight slanted through the thin upper story of the stately loblollies. The ocean was invisible, its presence a few thousand yards away suggested only by the muffled sound of surf and the sand on the forest floor.

At first the only mammals I sighted were a few domesticated species—a silver-mantled stroller, a golden-maned biker, and a pair of red-crested joggers. Then, suddenly, I saw a pine branch dip heavily like a trampoline, and a moment

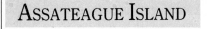

A commonplace sight at Assateague, black skimmers *(above)* fly inches from the water's surface, their lowered bills slicing through the water. When the skimmer's bill finally makes contact with a fish, it instantly snaps shut.

silhouetted against the blue sky, is a vision that few people can resist. "They tell you not to feed or pet them, but it's almost impossible not to," an unchastened visitor said. Staffers say that kicks and bites often result, and that one or two beggar ponies die each year when they amble into the path of a car.

They are believed to have descended from horses grazed on the island by seventeenth-century colonists evading taxes. More romantic legends tell of horses swimming ashore from shipwrecked galleons but historians, alas, have found no evidence supporting this.

It surprises many people to learn that the roughly 150 Chincoteague refuge ponies are owned by the town of Chincoteague's volunteer firemen. Every July the firefighters turn cowboy and round them up, swim them across the narrow channel separating Assateague and Chincoteague, and auction off the year's foals. The adults are returned to the refuge, where they forage on natural grass year-round and find water in the numerous pools. Another 150 ponies owned by the National Park Service patrol the Maryland side.

In summer, cattle egrets often perch on the backs of the ponies like jockeys and snatch insects off their coats. When the biting flies become unbearable, the ponies do the sensible thing: they take a dip in the surf.

Dunlins, among the hardiest of shorebirds, patrol Assateague's sandbars during the chilly winter *(below)*.

GRAYS
HARBOR
NWR

SKAGIT
WILDLIFE
AREA

OLYMPIC
NP

WASHINGTON

OREGON

MALHEUR NWR

HART MTN REFUGE

IDAHO

SNAKE RIVER
BIRDS OF PREY AREA

KLAMATH
BASIN
REFUGES

SHELDON NWR

NEVADA

PT. REYES/
FARALLON
ISLANDS

CALIFORNIA

JOSHUA TREE NM

GLACIER NP

MONTANA

J. CLARK SALYER NWR

NORTH DAKOTA

THEODORE ROOSEVELT NP

YELLOWSTONE NP

GRAND TETON NP

WYOMING

SOUTH DAKOTA

WIND CAVE NP

UTAH

ROCKY MOUNTAIN NP

MT. EVANS
WILDERNESS AREA

COLORADO

NEBRASKA

PLATTE
RIVER

KANSAS

QUIVIRA NWR

ARIZONA

SAGUARO NM

CHIRICAHUA
MOUNTAINS

NEW MEXICO

BOSQUE DEL APACHE NWR

CARLSBAD CAVERNS NP

OKLAHOMA

WICHITA MOUNTAINS NWR

TEXAS

ALASKA

DENALI NP

McNEIL RIVER
STATE SANCTUARY

PRIBILOF
ISLANDS

HAWAII

MOLOKINI ISLET

ARANSAS NWR

SANTA ANA
NWR

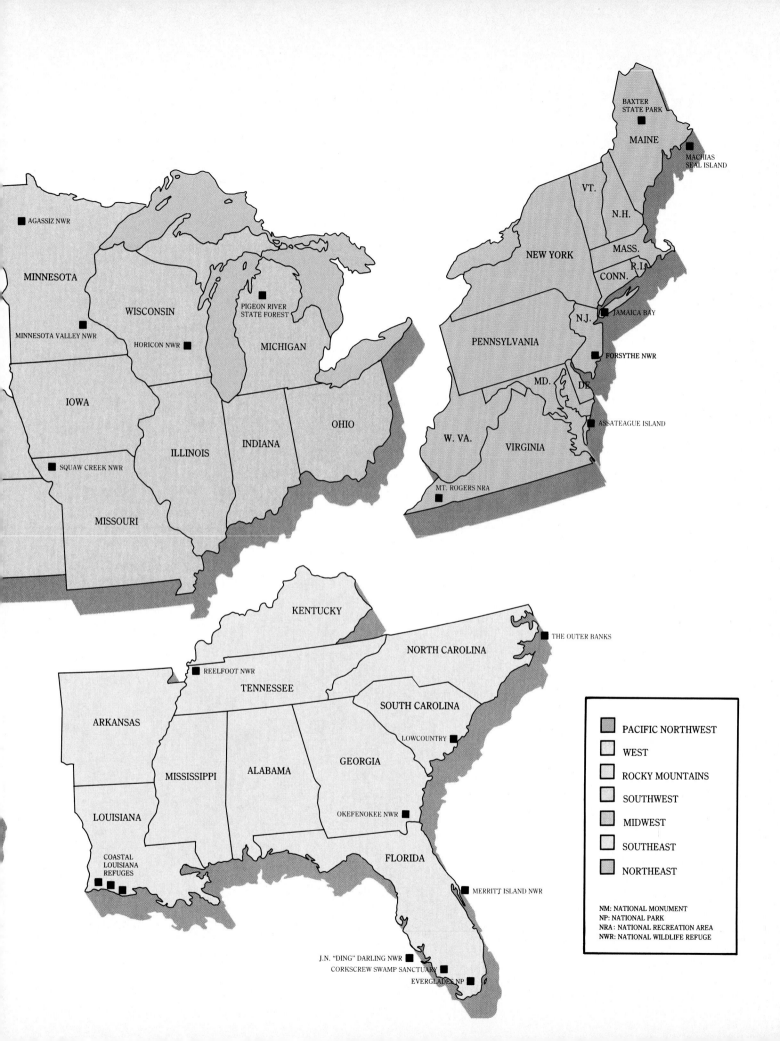

AGASSIZ NWR

MINNESOTA

WISCONSIN

MINNESOTA VALLEY NWR

HORICON NWR

PIGEON RIVER
STATE FOREST

MICHIGAN

IOWA

ILLINOIS

INDIANA

OHIO

SQUAW CREEK NWR

MISSOURI

BAXTER
STATE PARK

MAINE

MACHIAS
SEAL ISLAND

VT.

N.H.

NEW YORK

MASS.

CONN.

R.I.

N.J.

JAMAICA BAY

PENNSYLVANIA

FORSYTHE NWR

MD.

DE.

W. VA.

VIRGINIA

ASSATEAGUE ISLAND

MT. ROGERS NRA

KENTUCKY

NORTH CAROLINA

THE OUTER BANKS

REELFOOT NWR

TENNESSEE

SOUTH CAROLINA

ARKANSAS

LOWCOUNTRY

MISSISSIPPI

ALABAMA

GEORGIA

LOUISIANA

OKEFENOKEE NWR

COASTAL
LOUISIANA
REFUGES

FLORIDA

MERRITT ISLAND NWR

J.N. "DING" DARLING NWR

CORKSCREW SWAMP SANCTUARY

EVERGLADES NP

PACIFIC NORTHWEST

WEST

ROCKY MOUNTAINS

SOUTHWEST

MIDWEST

SOUTHEAST

NORTHEAST

NM: NATIONAL MONUMENT
NP: NATIONAL PARK
NRA: NATIONAL RECREATION AREA
NWR: NATIONAL WILDLIFE REFUGE

FOR MORE INFORMATION

AGASSIZ NWR
State Aid Hwy. 7
Middle River, MN 56737
(218) 449-4115
Directions: From Thief River Falls take Hwy. 32 north to Holt and turn east on County Road 7. It's about 11 miles to refuge headquarters.
Seasons: Waterfowl migrate south in late Sept. By Nov., only 13 species of birds remain for the winter. However, 274 species have been identified on the refuge since 1937. Moose and white-tailed deer may be seen year round.
Features: 100 foot observation tower; 4 mile auto drive.
Size: 61,487 acres

ARANSAS NWR
P.O. Box 100
Austwell, TX 77950
(512) 286-3559
Directions: Go north from Rockport on Hwy. 35, turn right on F.M. 774, then follow refuge signs.
Seasons: Call ahead in Oct. and Mar. to be sure cranes are present. Refuge open daily sunrise to sunset, visitor center 7:30-4:30 daily except Christmas Day.
Features: The visitor center has information on boat tours. Six walking trails branch out from the loop road, and an excellent self-guiding leaflet describes the main route. Organized youth groups can reserve campsites. Insect repellent a must.
Size: 54,829 acres

ASSATEAGUE ISLAND
See Assateague Island National Seashore and Chincoteague NWR.

ASSATEAGUE ISLAND NATIONAL SEASHORE
National Park Service
Route 2, Box 294
Berlin, MD 21811
(301) 641-1441
Directions: The entrance to Assateague National Seashore is an hour north of Chincoteague, Va. via Berlin, Md., and Maryland routes #113, 376, and 611. From Washington, DC, take US 50 east to US 13 south to Hwy. 175 east to Chincoteague.
Seasons: Open year round. Fee: $3 per car. Visitor centers serving both the Md. and Va. ends of the island are open 8:30-5.
Features: Wild ponies. Summertime interpretive activities and self-guided nature trails. Camping.
Size: 37 miles long

BAXTER STATE PARK
64 Balsam Drive
Millinocket, ME 04462
(207) 723-5140
Directions: Exit I-95 at Medway, head west to Millinocket on Rte. 157 and look for the McDonald's. Next to it is park headquarters. Park entrance is 18 miles north of the headquarters.
Seasons: The park is open for camping from May 15 to Oct. 15 and from Dec. 1 to Mar. 31. Headquarters is open 8-5 seven days a week from Memorial Day to Labor Day. After Labor Day, 8-5 M-F. Park hours vary with the season.
Features: Winter camping.
Size: 201,018 acres

BENTSEN RIO GRANDE VALLEY STATE PARK
P.O. Box 988
Mission, TX 78572
(512) 585-1107
Directions: From McAllen take Expressway 83 west to exit loop 374, left on FM 2062 to park entrance.
Seasons: Winter months best for birdwatching. Fee. Call ahead to ask about availability of campsites. Take insect repellent!
Features: Chachalaca, green jay, and bobcat in residence.
Size: 588 acres

BOSQUE del APACHE NWR
P.O. Box 1246
Socorro, NM 87801
(505) 835-1828
Directions: Located 93 miles south of Albuquerque. From Socorro take I-25 to San Antonio exit #139, then Route 380 east to Route 1 (at the Owl Cafe) and right (south) eight miles to the refuge.
Seasons: Wildlife present year-round but the best time to visit is between late Nov. and early Feb. Visitor center open daily except during summer when it is closed on weekends.
Features: The 15-mile auto tour is open one hour before sunrise and closed one hour after sunset. Fee: $2 per vehicle. Walking trails: Marsh Walk—3/4 mile, Bosque Trail—1 3/4 miles.
Size: 57,000 acres

CAPE HATTERAS NATIONAL SEASHORE
Rte. 1, Box 675
Manteo, NC 27954
(919) 473-2111
Directions: From Manteo, take US 64 east to Whalebone Junction. Turn right on NC 12, which runs the length of the seashore.
Seasons: Visitor center open year-round (9-6 summer, 9-5 winter). Campgrounds and some visitor facilities close during the winter.
Size: 45 square miles

CAPE ROMAIN NWR
Route 1, Box 191
Awendaw, SC 29429
(803) 928-3368
Directions: From US 17 at Awendaw, turn east on Sewee Road and follow signs to headquarters and boat landing.
Seasons: Large flocks of waterfowl present in winter. Shorebird and songbird migration peaks in Apr. American oystercatchers abundant in winter. Wood storks present in summer and fall. Brown pelican and wading bird rookeries active in spring and summer. Loggerhead sea turtles nest May through Aug. Mosquitoes abundant in warmer months. Visitor center open weekdays, 8:30-5.
Features: All-day boat trip to Bulls Island. Call the refuge (803) 928-3368 or boat operator (803) 884-0448 for schedule. Remaining areas of refuge accessible by private boat, but subject to seasonal closings to protect nesting species.
Capers Island accessible by private boat only with permit from South Carolina Wildlife and Marine Resources Department: (803) 795-6350

CARLSBAD CAVERNS NATIONAL PARK
3225 National Parks Hwy.
Carlsbad, NM 88220
(505) 785-2232
Directions: Take Hwy. 62-180 from Carlsbad south 20 miles to Whites City, then follow signs.
Seasons: Call ahead spring and fall to be sure bats are there. Wear sturdy non-slip shoes and a light jacket (cave temperature is in mid-50's all year).
Features: Fee to tour caverns. Lantern tour of undeveloped new cave by reservation. Other caves open by permit to qualified spelunkers. "Bat breakfast" in mid-Aug. to watch dawn flight. Call for exact date.
Size: 46,755 acres

CHINCOTEAGUE NWR
U.S. Fish and Wildlife Service
P.O. Box 62
Chincoteague, VA 23336
(804) 336-6122
Directions: Chincoteague NWR adjoins Chincoteague, Va., 10 miles east of US Hwy. #13 on the Maryland-Virginia eastern shore.
Seasons: Open year round. Fee: $3 per car. Visitor centers serving both the Md. and Va. ends of the island are open 8:30-5.

Features: Wild ponies, Delmarva squirrels. Summertime interpretive activities and self-guided nature trails. Camping.

CHIRICAHUA NATIONAL MONUMENT
Dos Cabezas Rte.
Box 6500
Willcox, AZ 85643
(602) 824-3560
Directions: From Tucson take I-10 east about 150 miles to Willcox. Go south on Hwy. 186 to 181. Turn left on 181 to headquarters.
Seasons: Peak times are mid-Apr. to mid-June for nesting birds. Midwinter snows can make mountain roads impassable, but park roads are plowed. Good footwear needed for rocky terrain, raingear for sudden showers. Temperature swings widely according to elevation.
Features: Camping is on a first-come basis. The maximum length for trailers is 26 feet. The 20 miles of trails are for day use only.
Size: 12,000 acres

COASTAL LOUISIANA REFUGES
Seasons: Songbird migration peaks in Apr. and Oct. Waterfowl concentrations peak in late fall and winter. Summer months are hot, humid, and buggy. Mid-winter weather can be blustery.
See Lacassine NWR, and Rockefeller Refuge, and Sabine NWR.

CORKSCREW SWAMP SANCTUARY
Rte. 6, Box 1875A
Sanctuary Road
Naples, FL 33964
(813) 657-3771
Directions: From I-75, take exit 17 and travel east on Rte. 846 for 15 miles to the refuge sign. Turn on Sanctuary Road (Rte. 849) and continue 1.5 miles to visitor center.
Seasons: Viewing alligators, turtles, and wading birds is best Dec.

through Apr. In years when storks nest, activity is usually underway by Mar. Call for up-to-date nesting information. Visitor center open 9-5.
Features: Trail open until sunset, but visitors must get to visitor center by 5 p.m. Fee.
Size: 10,560 acres

CUSTER STATE PARK
HRC 83, Box 70
Custer, SD 57730
(605) 255-4515
Directions: An hour's drive south of Rapid City.
Seasons: No winter visitor services.
Size: 73,000 acres

J.N. "DING" DARLING NWR
P.O. Drawer B
Sanibel, FL 33957
(813) 472-1100
Directions: From Ft. Myers, take Hwy. 41 south to Rte. 865, then southwest on Rte. 867 to the Sanibel Causeway (toll). On Sanibel Island, turn right at the first intersection after the causeway and drive 2.5 miles on Periwinkle Way. Turn right on Palm Ridge Road for .5 mile. Go straight on Sanibel-Captiva Road for 2.3 miles. Visitor center is on the right.
Seasons: Spoonbills: Feb. through Aug. Songbird migration: mid-Apr. Nesting terns, pelicans, mottled ducks, and wading birds: spring and summer. Ospreys, night herons, and alligators: year-round. Open daylight hours. Fee: $3 per vehicle.
Features: Sanibel is a tropical island 3 miles off the Florida mainland in the Gulf of Mexico.
Size: 5,014 acres

DENALI NATIONAL PARK AND PRESERVE
P.O. Box 9
Denali Park, AK 99755
(907) 683-2294

Directions: Park entrance is on Hwy. 3, about 237 miles north of Anchorage.
Seasons: June usually brings fewer visitors than July and Aug. The tundra turns beautiful tones of yellow, orange, and red in late Aug. and early Sept. Fee: $3 per person.
Features: Tundra and spruce taiga, as well as glaciers, gravel-banked rivers, and small lakes. Access is by shuttle buses (6 a.m. to 11 p.m.) along an unpaved road. Make campground and backcountry reservations at the visitor center.
Size: 5,696,000 acres

EVERGLADES NATIONAL PARK
P.O. Box 279
Homestead, FL 33030
(305) 247-6211
Directions: From the junction of I-95 and Hwy. 1, take Rte. 9336 southwest 12 miles to headquarters. Flamingo is 38 miles past headquarters on the main road. Shark Valley—on Hwy. 41, approximately 30 miles west of Miami. Everglades City—west on Hwy. 41, 65 miles from Miami, or east on Hwy. 41, 30 miles fron. Naples, then south on Rte. 29, 5 miles to the ranger station.
Seasons: Many species present year-round. Viewing alligators, anhingas, and turtles best from Dec. through Apr. Fee.
Features: Separate fees for boat tours at Flamingo and Everglades City and for tram tours at Shark Valley.
Size: 1.4 million acres

FARALLON ISLANDS
San Francisco Bay NWR
P.O. Box 524
Newark, CA 94560
(415) 792-0222
Directions: 25 miles west of the Golden Gate Bridge. Monthly sailing trips by the San Francisco Bay Chapter of the Oceanic Society. Fee. Visitors are not allowed to go

ashore. For reservations call (415) 441-5970.

EDWIN B. FORSYTHE NWR
P.O. Box 72
Oceanville, NJ 08231
(609) 652-1665
Directions: From Atlantic City take Route 30 to Absecon, then Route 9 for about 4.5 miles to Great Creek Road in Oceanville. Turn right to refuge headquarters.
Seasons: Open sunrise to sunset all year. Insect repellent is recommended in summer.
Features: Brigantine Division is the only public use area. Footpaths and an 8-mile wildlife drive offer exceptional opportunities for wildlife viewing. Two observation towers. Self-guided tour leaflet.
Size: 36,000 acres

GLACIER NATIONAL PARK
West Glacier, MT 59936
(406) 888-5441
Directions: Park is reached via Hwy. 2 and Hwy. 89.
Seasons: Headquarters open weekdays 8-4:30. June through Sept. is the best visiting time. Winter travel ranges from chancy to impossible.
Features: Bordering Canada and contiguous with that country's Waterton Lakes National Park, Glacier is part of the unique International Peace Park. More than 700 miles of hiking and horse trails. Dozens of small glaciers.
Size: 1,013,598 acres

GRAND TETON NATIONAL PARK
P.O. Drawer 170
Moose, WY 83012
(307) 733-2880
Directions: In northwest Wyoming, 10 miles north of Jackson at US 89 & 287.
Seasons: Snow blankets the park from late Nov. through Apr. averaging 3 to 5 feet in the valley and 10 to 15 feet in the Teton

Range. Moose Visitor Center remains open year-round except for Christmas Day. The Colter Bay Visitor Center closes Sept. 30 to mid-May.
Features: Skiing, backpacking, boating, and mountaineering. Ranger-led snowshoe hikes (snowshoes provided, reservations required) twice weekly, late Dec. through mid-Mar.
Size: 3l0,521 acres
See also National Elk Refuge.

GRAYS HARBOR NWR
c/o Nisqually NWR
100 Brown Farm Road
Olympia, WA 98506
(206) 753-9467
Directions: Take Hwy. 101 along the coast to Hoquiam. Take Hwy. 109 just beyond the Hoquiam High School, then follow the Paulson Road toward the airport, Bowerman Field.
Seasons: Shorebird numbers usually peak about Apr. 25; numbers are much lower before Apr. 15 and after Apr. 30. Yet shorebirds are present throughout the year, and other wild animals are also present seasonally.
Features: Grays Harbor NWR was authorized by Congress in 1988 and land acquisition will not be completed for several years. Until then the area is owned by the Port of Grays Harbor and the city of Hoquiam. A visitor center, boardwalks, and displays are planned for 1991 and later.
Size: 1,800 acres

HART MOUNTAIN NATIONAL ANTELOPE REFUGE
Headquarters
Box 111
Lakeview, OR 97630
(503) 947-3315
Directions: From Lakeview to Plush, and then another 24 miles to headquarters. Also accessible via a 28-mile dirt road from Frenchglen

on the east, or 23 miles of dirt road from Adel on the south.
Seasons: Fawns in May and June. Mating in Aug. and Sept. Deep snow possible in winter; rain may make the roads impassable in spring.
Features: Camping permitted. Take drinking water.
Size: 241,000 acres

HORICON NWR
W4279 Headquarters Road
Mayville, WI 53050
(414) 387-2658
Directions: From Madison, take Hwy. 151 north to State Hwy. 49, go east for about 6 miles to County Road Z. Go right on Z and south 4 miles to headquarters.
Seasons: Trails are open from sunrise to sunset. Hikers and cross-country ski enthusiasts have six miles of trails off Hwy. 49 in the north end of the federal area. Hikers and bicyclists can use the Main Dike Road from mid-Apr. to Sept. 15.
Features: Thousands of migrating waterfowl during spring and fall. One of the country's largest freshwater cattail marshes.
Size: 21,000 acres

JAMAICA BAY WILDLIFE REFUGE
Gateway NRA
Floyd Bennett Field
Brooklyn, NY 11234
(718) 474-0613
Directions: Refuge is reachable by the IND subway line and a one-mile walk from Broad Channel station or by car via the Belt Parkway and Crossbay Blvd. Watch for refuge sign after you cross North Channel Bridge.
Seasons: Trails open 8:30-5 every day. Spring and fall are prime birding seasons.
Features: 1 3/4-mile gravel walking trail around 45-acre West Pond.
Size: 9,155 acres

JOSHUA TREE NATIONAL MONUMENT
74485 National Monument Dr.
Twentynine Palms, CA 92277
(619) 367-7511
Directions: Approximately three hours east of Los Angeles, via I-10 and Rte. 62 east of Cabazon.
Seasons: The Joshua tree blooms in Mar./Apr., but not every year. Wildflowers best in Mar./Apr. Spring is the best time to observe snakes.
Features: From headquarters at Twentynine Palms on Rte. 62, the road runs south toward I-10. Take water, firewood (dead wood is protected), and warm clothes—even summer nights are nippy.
Size: 559,960 acres

KLAMATH BASIN NATIONAL WILDLIFE REFUGES
U.S. Fish and Wildlife Service
Rte. 1, Box 74
Tulelake, CA 96134
(916) 667-2231
Directions: From San Francisco, Tule Lake is an eight hour drive up I-5 to Weed and northeast on Hwy. 97, then east just past Dorris on Rte. 161. Headquarters is five miles west of the town of Tulelake, 1/2 mile south of the end of East-West Road.
Seasons: Wildlife abounds on the six refuges of this complex at all times of the year; peak waterfowl numbers occur mid-Nov.; wintering bald eagles have exceeded 600. Refuges are open sunrise to sunset.
Features: Auto tour routes available at Tule Lake and Lower Klamath refuges; canoe trail at Upper Klamath refuge; visitor center at Tule Lake. No overnight camping, but five campground/trailer parks nearby.
Lower Klamath: 51,000+ acres
Tule Lake: 38,000+ acres

LACASSINE NWR
HCR 63, Box 186
Lake Arthur, LA 70549
(318) 774-5923
Directions: The refuge is 22 miles southwest of Jennings. Follow Rte. 26 south to Lake Arthur, then take SR 14 west 7 miles to SR 3056 (Lowry Road). Travel 5 miles south to headquarters. Auto access to Lacassine Pool is off SR 14, several miles west of the headquarters turnoff. Follow refuge signs.
Seasons: Headquarters open daylight hours. Some areas may be closed Oct. 16 to Feb. 28 to protect wintering waterfowl.
Size: 32,624 acres

MACHIAS SEAL ISLAND
Maine
Directions: Located in the Bay of Fundy about 13 miles from Cutler. Boat service is available from Jonesport off Rte. 1.

MALHEUR NWR
HC 72, Box 245
Princeton, OR 97721
(503) 493-2825
Directions: From Burns, take Rte. 78 east, then Rte. 205 south 25 miles to refuge sign, then left 5 miles to headquarters.
Seasons: Spring waterfowl migration peaks in Mar. Shorebirds arrive in Apr., songbirds in May.
Size: 185,000 acres

MCNEIL RIVER STATE SANCTUARY
Alaska Dept. of Fish and Game
333 Raspberry Road
Anchorage, AK 99518-1599
(907) 267-2179
Directions: McNeil River is about 200 miles southwest of Anchorage. Access is primarily by plane. Flights to McNeil can be chartered from Homer for about $250 round trip.
Seasons: Access to McNeil River between July 1 and Aug. 25 (when bears are at the falls) is by permit only. Permits are issued by a

lottery on Apr. 15. Applications are available from Alaska Department of Fish and Game.
Features: Large numbers of Alaskan brown bears.

MERRITT ISLAND NWR
P.O. Box 6504
Titusville, FL 32780
(305) 867-0667
Directions: From Orlando, take the Beeline (S.R. 50) Expressway east to I-95, north to Rte. 406 (exit 80), and follow 406 to the refuge.
Seasons: Refuge open daylight hours, 7 days a week. Perimeter closings and restrictions apply within 3 days of space launches. Visitor center open 8-4:30 weekdays, 9-5 weekends. Closed on Sundays in the summer. Mosquitoes abundant in summer.
Features: Saltwater lagoons, uplands, marshes, and swamps.
Size: 134,143 acres

MILE HI/RAMSEY CANYON PRESERVE
RR 1, Box 84
Hereford, AZ 85615-9738
(602) 378-2785
Directions: From Tucson, take I-10 east and Hwy. 90 south to Sierra Vista. Pick up Hwy. 92 east of Sierra Vista and go south 10 miles to the turnoff. Turn right and drive 4 miles to the Mile Hi cabins.
Seasons: Hours are 8-5 every day. Weekdays tend to be less crowded except Mar.-Sept.
Features: Fee: $3. No fee for Nature Conservancy members. The 14 parking spaces for day visitors require reservations for weekends and holidays. No trailers. Reservations must be made 9 to 14 months in advance for the six housekeeping cabins. No picnicking, pets, collecting, or camping.
Size: 300 acres

MINNESOTA VALLEY NWR
4101 E. 80th
Bloomington, MN 55424
(612) 854-5900
Directions: From I-494 take the 34th Ave. exit south to 80th St., turn left on 80th St. and follow it .5 miles to headquarters.
Seasons: Open year round.
Features: An urban green belt along a 34-mile stretch of the Minnesota River from Fort Snelling to Jordon. Trails for hiking, horseback riding, biking, cross-country skiing, and snowmobiling. A visitor center is scheduled to open in 1990.
Size: 7,000 acres

MOLOKINI ISLET
Maui, Hawaii
Directions: Three miles off the coast of Maui.
Seasons: Whale watching is Jan. through Apr. Cruises leave from docks at Lahaina.
Features: Consult local dive shops, which offer good maps of snorkeling locations around the island and will often book cruises to Molokini. Or contact the Aloha Activity Center (808) 667-9564.

MT. EVANS WILDERNESS AREA
National Forest Service
Clear Creek Ranger District
Idaho Springs, CO 80452
(303) 567-2901
Directions: Exit I-70 at #240 to Idaho Springs; take Rte. 103 to the junction of 103 and Rte. 5; then take Rte. 5 on to the summit.
Seasons: Road usually open all the way to the top between late June and Labor Day. Snow likely except during July and Aug.

MT. ROGERS NATIONAL RECREATION AREA
Jefferson National Forest
210 Franklin Road, SW
Roanoke, VA 24001
(703) 783-5196

Directions: 10 miles east of Marion, Va. on Rte. 16.
Features: Approximately 300 wildlife species in Jefferson National Forest. Offers remoteness, naturalness, and opportunities for solitude. Several trails.
Size: 12,985 acres

NATIONAL ELK REFUGE
P.O. Box C
Jackson, WY 83001
(307) 733-9212
Directions: In northwest Wyoming, 10 miles north of Jackson at US 89 & 287.
Seasons: Snow blankets the park from late Nov. through Apr. averaging 3 to 5 feet in the valley and 10 to 15 feet in the Teton Range. Moose Visitor Center remains open year-round except for Christmas Day. The Colter Bay Visitor Center closes Sept. 30 to mid-May.
Seasons: Little wildlife is seen at the refuge during the summer, but more than 7,000 elk are there from Nov. through Apr.
Features: Sleigh rides to view the elk from late Dec. to late Mar.
Size: 24,000 acres

OKEFENOKEE NWR
Route 2, Box 338
Folkston, GA 31537
(912) 496-3331
Directions: Three main entrances lead into the refuge—Suwannee Canal Recreation Area (12 miles southwest of Folkston), Stephen C. Foster State Park (17 miles northeast of Fargo), and Okefenokee Swamp Park (8 miles south of Waycross). Fee.
Seasons: Wildlife abounds year-round. Sandhill cranes, ducks, and other migratory birds are numerous Nov. through Mar. Otter are seen during cold weather and alligators are active in summer.
Features: Guided boat tours, boardwalks, hiking trails, and wilderness canoe camping trips by

permit from headquarters.
Size: 396,000 acres

OLYMPIC NATIONAL PARK
600 East Park Avenue
Port Angeles, WA 98362
(206) 452-4501
Directions: US 101 leads to the park with numerous spur roads leading to the interior. To camp the western beaches take US 101 to the Smokehouse restaurant near Forks, and follow the signs west. When the road forks, take either the Rialto Beach route north or the La Push route south, depending on which side of the Quillayute River you want to explore.
Seasons: Visitor centers at Port Angeles and at the Hoh rain forest. Open 9-7 July and Aug., 9-5 other months.
Features: Scheduled campfires and nature walks. Nature trails start behind the visitor center. To sample the peninsula's diversity, visit the Hoh rain forest, Hurricane Ridge, and Ruby Beach. Horseback riding, mountaineering, winter sports, fishing, and 18 campgrounds.
Size: 922,000 acres

THE OUTER BANKS
North Carolina
Seasons: Summers are hot, humid, and may harbor biting insects. Winters can be blustery. Best months to visit are Apr.-May and Oct.-Nov.
See Cape Hatteras National Seashore and Pea Island NWR.
Also on the Outer Banks:
Alligator River NWR
P.O. Box 1969
Manteo, NC 27954
(919) 473-1131
Cedar Island National Refuge
Rt. 1, Box N-2
Swanquarter, NC 27885
(919) 225-2511
Currituck NWR
P.O. Box 1969
Manteo, NC 27954
(919) 473-1131

PEA ISLAND NWR

P.O. Box 1969
Manteo, NC 27954
(919) 473-1131
Directions: From Nags Head, take NC Rt. 12 south. Cross Oregon Inlet onto Hatteras Island. The refuge is the north 13 miles of Hatteras Island. Pea Island refuge lies within Cape Hatteras National Seashore.
Seasons: Open daily, daylight hours; office open 9-4, M-F, Apr.-Sept.
Features: Barrier island habitat with man-made waterfowl impoundments.
Size: 5,915 acres

PIGEON RIVER COUNTRY STATE FOREST

Michigan Department of Natural Resources
9966 Twin Lakes Road
Vanderbilt, MI 49795
(517) 983-4101
Directions: Take Hwy. 75 to Vanderbilt, then go five miles east of Vanderbilt.
Seasons: Best viewing time is the end of Apr. through May and from late Aug. through Oct.
Features: Seven campgrounds.
Size: 95,000 acres

PLATTE RIVER-BIG BEND REACH

Nebraska
Directions: Big Bend area encompasses approximately 60 miles of Platte River roughly from Grand Island to Lexington.
Seasons: The best time to see cranes is mid-Mar. One of the best places is near Kearney.
Features: Hwy. 2 northwest from Grand Island is both scenic and lonesome. For crane information, contact the Platte River Whooping Crane Maintenance Trust, 2550 North Diers Avenue, Suite H, Grand Island, NE 68803
(308) 384-4633 or

The Nebraska Game and Parks Commission, P.O. Box 30370, Lincoln, NE 68503.

PRIBILOF ISLANDS

Alaska Dept. of Fish and Game
P.O. Box 1030
Dillingham, AK 99576
(907) 842-1013
Directions: Flights connect Anchorage and St. Paul. A smaller plane connects St. Paul with St. George on Fri. Visitors must stay in hotels with reservations pre-arranged through tour companies that travel to the Pribilofs. Contact Exploration Holidays (1-800-426-0600) or Midnight Sun Tours (1-800-544-2235). Bus/van transportation to the bird and seal rookeries is also arranged through tours.
Seasons: June, July, and Aug. are peak times for seabirds and marine mammals.
Size: St. Paul is 44 square miles, St. George is smaller.

PT. REYES NATIONAL SEASHORE

Pt. Reyes, CA 94956
(415) 663-1092
Directions: 35 miles northwest of San Francisco on Hwy. 1.
Seasons: Year round.
Features: Bear Valley Interpretive Center has 250 exhibits and 140 specimens of native plants. A working seismograph measures the San Andreas fault movement.
Size: 100 square miles of seashore

QUIVIRA NWR

Rte. Three, Box 48A
Stafford, KS 67578
(316) 486-2393
Directions: From Hutchinson, take Rte. 50 west to Zenith, then to Zenith Road right 8 miles (continuing as it becomes dirt) to headquarters.
Seasons: Bird migrations in fall and spring. Bald and golden eagles Nov.-Mar. In summer, Swainson's hawk and Mississippi kite.

Features: No developed trails, but hikers can use access roads, levees or other paths.
Size: 21,820 acres

REELFOOT NWR

Rt. 2, Hwy. 157
Union City, TN 38261
(901) 538-2481
Directions: From Tiptonville, take Rte. 22 east about 15 miles. Turn left on SR 157, continue 1 mile to center.
Seasons: Refuge visitor center open 8-4, M-F. Isom and North units closed Oct. 15-Mar. 15 and Grassy Island unit closed Nov. 15-Mar. 15. (Wildlife drive open all year.) State park visitor center open 8-4:30, M-F. 8-6, Sat. & Sun. Jan. 2-Mar. 15. Eagle tours (fee) provided by Reelfoot State Park depart daily, 10 am, Dec. 1-21 and Jan. 2-Mar. 15. For reservations, call (901) 253-9652.
Size: 13,000 acres

ROCKEFELLER WILDLIFE REFUGE

Rte. 1, Box 20-B
Grand Chenier, LA 70643
(318) 538-2276
Directions: Midway between Grand Chenier and Pecan Island on SR 82. The refuge is about 50 miles southeast of Lake Charles.
Seasons: Headquarters open 7-4, M-F. Refuge is open Mar. 1 to Nov. 30.
Features: Travel is by boat.
Size: 76,042 acres

ROCKY MOUNTAIN NATIONAL PARK

Estes Park, CO 80517-8397
(303) 586-2371
Directions: On US 34. Air, rail, or bus via Denver.
Seasons: Open all year, though Trail Ridge Road (US 34) is closed Oct. to June.
Size: 265,193 acres

THEODORE ROOSEVELT NATIONAL PARK

Box 7
Medora, ND 58645
(701) 623-4466
Directions: Two units of the park are near I-94 in western North Dakota. The north unit is 15 miles south of Wadford City.
Seasons: Park is open year round.
Features: Bison, wild horse, elk, mule deer, prairie dog.
Size: 70,416 acre park in three units

SABINE NWR

Hwy. 27 South
3000 Main St.
Hackberry, LA 70645
(318) 762-3816
Directions: From Lake Charles, take I-10 west to Sulphur, then south on Rte. 27 to refuge signs.
Seasons: Headquarters open 7-4, M-F and noon-4, Sat.-Sun. Refuge open daylight hours.
Features: Largest waterfowl refuge on the Gulf Coast.
Size: 142,846 acres

SAGUARO NATIONAL MONUMENT

3693 So. Old Spanish Trail
Tucson, AZ 85730-5699
(602) 883-6366 (West)
(602) 296-8576 (East)
Directions: The Monument is on two tracts near Tucson. To reach the Tucson mountain district leave Tucson on the Speedway west to its end, then right at the "T" seven miles to the sign. To reach the Rincon mountain district, take the Speedway east to Harrison, right to the Old Spanish Trail and left to monument signs.
Features: Scenic roads and hiking trails. Wilderness hiking and camping are available with permits only at the Rincon mountain district. Always take water on extended hikes. Fees.
Size: 83,576 acres

J. CLARK SALYER NWR
P.O. Box 66
Upham, ND 58789
(701) 768-2548

Directions: From Minot, take Rte. 83 north 25 miles to Upham turnoff, then gravel road east 27 miles to Upham, then Rte. 14 north 2 miles to headquarters.

Seasons: Fall offers the most awesome waterfowl numbers. Spring manages about half the fall volume, but many of the birds are in handsome breeding plumage. From June through Aug. broods of young waterfowl are on parade and during Aug. as many as 200,000 ducks come to the refuge to molt.

Size: 58,700 acres

SANTA ANA NWR
Rte. 2, Box 202A
Alamo, TX 78516
(512) 787-7861

Directions: From McAllen take Expressway 83 east to Alamo, then south on FM 907 to end of road at Hwy. 281. Turn left and go about .3 mile to refuge sign.

Seasons: Foot access sunrise to sunset daily. Visitor center open 8-4:30 weekdays, 9-4:30 weekends, closed Thanksgiving, Christmas, New Year's.

Features: Tropical birds and sub-tropical woodlands. Foot access sunrise to sunset daily. Tram (fee) with guide operates Nov.-Apr. Take insect repellent!

Size: 2,080 acres

SANTEE COASTAL RESERVE AND WASHO RESERVE
P.O. Box 37
McClellanville, SC 29458
(803) 546-8665

Directions:
Santee/Washo Reserves: From US 17, turn east on Santee Road. The turnoff is the first paved road south of the Santee River bridge. It is about 17 miles south of Georgetown. Follow the dirt road to Santee Gun Club Road and turn left. Drive about 2 miles to the Washo

trailhead, on the right, or the Santee office, on the left.

Seasons: Open 9-5 weekdays from Mar. 1 to Oct. 31. Refuge closed to visitors Nov. 1 through Feb. 28.

SHELDON NWR
Headquarters
Box 111
Lakeview, OR 97630
(503) 947-3315

Directions: From Reno, take Hwy. 80 to Winnemucca, then 95 to 140. There are entrances to Sheldon off Hwy. 140, 65 miles from Lakeview on the west side; 46 miles from Cedarville, Ca; others from Summit Lake and Denio.

Seasons: Fawns in May and June. Mating in Aug. and Sept. Deep snow possible in winter; rain may make the roads impassable in spring.

Features: A paved road, Hwy. 140, transects Sheldon. Better viewing is from the refuge's own dirt roads to the south, but they are very hard on tires so drive slowly. Camping permitted. Take drinking water.

Size: 575,000 acres

SKAGIT WILDLIFE AREA
Nature Conservancy
1601 Second Avenue
Suite 910
Seattle, WA 98104
(206) 624-9623
or:
Department of Game
Nongame Wildlife Program
Evergreen State College
3109 Seminar Bldg.
Olympia, WA 98505
(206) 754-1449

Directions: Take I-5 north from Seattle. Take Hwy. 20 east to see eagles. Take Hwy. 20 west to the Skagit Flats geese and swans.

Seasons: The best time to see geese, swans, and eagles is winter. The Nature Conservancy asks you to wait until after 10:00 a.m. (when the eagles have finished eating) to put in rafts or canoes at

Marblemount, the approved entry point.

Features: The best eagle viewing is from along Hwy. 20 near the towns of Rockport, Marblemount, and Concrete.

Size: 1,500 acres

SNAKE RIVER BIRDS OF PREY AREA
Bureau of Land Management
District Office
3948 Development Ave.
Boise, ID 83705
(208) 334-1582

Directions: There are several automobile access sites to the canyon rim or to the river. The easiest is via Kuna and Hwy. 69 to a graded dirt road to an observation area at Dedication Point and the river at Swan Falls Dam. Access to the river is also available at Brunneau and Grandview.

Seasons: Mar. through June is nesting season for birds.

Features: Several outfitters in Boise offer rafting trips into the canyon. Binoculars or a spotting scope are necessary to watch the raptors.

Size: 483,000 acres

SOUTH CAROLINA LOWCOUNTRY
See Cape Romain NWR, and Santee Coastal Reserve.

SQUAW CREEK NWR
Box 101
Mound City, MO 64470
(816) 442-3187

Directions: Headquarters is just west of I-29 on Hwy. 159 (Exit 79).

Seasons: Eagle Day is celebrated every year, usually Sat. and Sun. of the first week in Dec. Peak waterfowl migration is mid-Oct. to mid-Nov.: 300,000 snow geese, 100,000 ducks, and 250 bald eagles. Call ahead for road conditions and waterfowl numbers.

Size: 6,900 acres

WICHITA MOUNTAINS REFUGE
Box 448
Indiahoma, OK 73552
(405) 429-3222

Directions: From Lawton, take Hwy. 62 west to Cache, then Hwy. 115 north to refuge (about 25 miles).

Seasons: Best times are Apr. through Nov. Refuge open 24 hours daily, office 8-4:30 weekdays, visitor center weekends 10-6, Mar.-Nov.

Features: Backcountry camping on limited reservation basis with fee. Campground is first-come, first-served (fee). Reserve ahead for popular elk-bugling tours mid-Sept. through mid-Oct.

Size: 59,000 acres

WIND CAVE NATIONAL PARK
Hot Springs, SD 57747
(605)745-4600

Directions: Wind Cave lies about an hour's drive south of Rapid City. Wind Cave and Custer State Park share a common boundary.

Seasons: Bison, prairie dogs, and pronghorn remain active throughout the day. Apr. through Oct. are the best times to visit.

Features: One-fourth forested and three-fourths grassland. Visitor services available in winter.

Size: 28,232 acres

YELLOWSTONE NATIONAL PARK
P.O. Box 168
Yellowstone National Park, WY 82190
(307) 344-7381

Directions: Yellowstone is about 80 miles south of Bozeman, Montana.

Seasons: Outstanding wildlife watching all year, but it's easiest to find the animals during the winter when they concentrate on their winter ranges. Winter visitors should come equipped for cold.

Size: 2,221,766 acres

INDEX

NF = National Forest
NM = National Monument
NP = National Park
NRA = National Recreation Area
NS = National Seashore
NWR = National Wildlife Refuge

**Library of Congress
Cataloging-in-Publication Data**

America's wildlife hideaways.

    Includes index.
        1. Zoology—United
States. 2. Natural areas—United
States. I. National Wildlife
Federation.
QL155.A57   1989   508.73
89-8290
ISBN 0-945051-08-5
ISBN 0-945051-12-3 (leatherbound)

CREDITS

Cover: Erwin and Peggy Bauer. **Back cover:** Stan Osolinski. **Page 1:** Johnny Johnson. **2-3:** Annie Griffiths Belt. **6-7:** Kim Heacox.

PACIFIC NORTHWEST

Pages 8-9: Johnny Johnson. **10:** Bill McRae. **10-11:** Johnny Johnson. **11 top:** John Shaw. **12-13:** Johnny Johnson. **13:** David C. Fritts. **14-15:** Johnny Johnson. **15 top:** Johnny Johnson; **bottom:** John Shaw. **16-17:** Jeff Foott. **17 bottom:** François Gohier. **18:** Stephen J. Krasemann/DRK Photo. **18-19:** Yogi Kaufman. **19 top:** Photography by Hinke/Sacilotto. **20-21 all:** Tom Walker. **22:** Dominique Braud. **23:** Steve Kaufman. **24-25 all:** Larry R. Ditto. **26:** Laura Riley. **27:** Joe and Carol McDonald. **28-29:** Glenn Van Nimwegen. **30-31 all:** Charles Krebs. **32:** Tom and Pat Leeson. **32-33:** Tom Algire. **34:** Art Wolfe. **34-35:** John Shaw. **36:** Art Wolfe. **36-37:** Charles Krebs.

WEST

Pages 38-39: Kevin Schafer. **40-41 all:** François Gohier. **42:** Kevin Schafer. **43:** Tupper Ansel Blake. **44:** Keith Szafranski. **45:** Tom and Pat Leeson. **46-47 all:** Jeffrey Rich. **48-49:** Kevin Schafer. **49 bottom:** Tupper Ansel Blake. **50:** Jeff Foott. **51:** Breck P. Kent. **52-53:** Stephen J. Krasemann/DRK Photo. **54-55 all:** William H. Mullins. **56-57:** © Stephen Kasper 1989. **58:** Steve Kaufman. **59:** © Stephen Kasper 1989. **60-61:** Tom Stack/Tom Stack and Associates. **61 top:** Ed Robinson/Tom Stack and Associates. **62-63 all:** François Gohier.

SOUTHWEST

Pages 64-65: John Shaw. **66:** Art Wolfe. **67 left:** George H.H. Huey; **right:** Jen and Des Bartlett/Bruce Coleman, Inc. **68 top:** George H.H. Huey; **bottom:** G.C. Kelley. **69:** George H.H. Huey. **70-71:** George H.H. Huey. **72 left:** George H.H. Huey; **top right:** G.C. Kelley; **bottom right:** Dr. Edward S. Ross. **73:** G.C. Kelley. **74 left:** C. Allan Morgan; **right:** G.C. Kelley. **75:** Robert P. Carr. **76-77:** Wendy Shattil and Bob Rozinski. **77 top:** Renee Lynn. **78:** C. Gable Ray. **79:** Larry R. Ditto. **80:** J. Scott Altenbach. **80-81:** Ronal C. Kerbo. **82-83 all:** Glenn Van Nimwegen. **84:** Wendell Metzen. **85:** Glenn Van Nimwegen. **86:** Jeff Foott. **87:** Frank Oberle. **88-90 all:** Wendy Shattil and Bob Rozinski. **91:** E.R. Degginger/Animals Animals. **92:** Stephen J. Krasemann/DRK Photo. **92-93:** Larry R. Ditto. **94:** John Shaw. **95:** Lou Jost.

ROCKY MOUNTAINS

Pages 96-97: Lynn M. Stone. **98:** Derek Hanson. **98-99:** Steve Kaufman. **100:** Stephen J. Krasemann/DRK Photo. **100-101:** Bill McRae. **101 top:** W.W. Lockwood. **103:** Stephen J. Krasemann/DRK Photo. **104-105:** Charles Krebs. **105 bottom:** Jeff Foott. **106:** Pat O'Hara/DRK Photo. **107:** Art Wolfe. **108-109 all:** Glenn Van Nimwegen. **110-111:** Steven Fuller. **111 top:** Breck P. Kent. **112:** Sharon Cummings. **113:** Rita Summers. **114-115:** Steven Fuller. **116-117 top:** John Gerlach/DRK Photo; **bottom:** Scott Nielsen/Imagery. **118 left:** Steve Kaufman. **118-119:** Steve Kaufman. **119 top:** Dominique Braud. **120 left:** Charles Krebs. **120-121:** John Shaw. **123:** Jerry Ferrara. **124 left:** Jeff Foott. **124-125:** David C. Fritts. **126-127:** Wendy Shattil and Bob Rozinski. **127 top:** Dominique Braud. **128 top:** Kent and Donna Dannen; **bottom:** Wendy Shattil and Bob Rozinski. **129:** Wendy Shattil and Bob Rozinski. **130 left:** John Cancalosi. **130-131:** W. Perry Conway.

MIDWEST

Pages 132-139 all: Dominique Braud. **140 left:** Scott W. Sharkey. **140-141:** Jim Brandenburg. **143:** Frank Oberle. **144:** Tim Davis. **145:** Frank Oberle. **146-149 all:** Mike Blair. **150 left:** Frank Oberle. **150-151:** Mike Blair. **152 left:** George J. Sanker/DRK Photo. **152-153:** Glenn Van Nimwegen. **153 bottom:** Jeffrey Rich. **154:** Daniel J. Cox. **155:** Carl R. Sams, II/M.L. Dembinsky, Jr. Photography Associates. **156-157:** Jim West. **157 top:** Robert P. Carr.

SOUTHEAST

Pages 158-159: Erwin and Peggy Bauer. **160:** Glenn Van Nimwegen. **160-161:** Breck P. Kent. **162 left:** Lynn M. Stone; **right:** Robert Villani. **163:** George J. Sanker/DRK Photo. **164 left:** Charles Krebs. **164-165:** Charles Krebs. **165 top:** Erwin and Peggy Bauer. **166 left:** Gail Shumway; **bottom right:** Stephen J. Krasemann/DRK Photo. **166-167:** M.P. Kahl/DRK Photo. **168-169:** Wendell Metzen. **169 top:** C. Gable Ray; **bottom:** Gail Shumway. **170-171:** Lynn M. Stone. **171 top:** Robert Villani. **172:** John Shaw. **173:** James H. Robinson. **174 all:** Wendell Metzen. **175:** Douglas Faulkner. **176 left:** Scott Nielsen/Imagery. **176-177:** David Muench. **177 right:** Frank Oberle. **178 left:** Jack Dermid. **178-179:** Wendell Metzen. **179 top:** Bill Weems. **180-181 all:** Jack Dermid. **182-183:** Wendell Metzen. **184:** Calvin Larsen/National Audubon Society Collection/PR. **185:** Bates Littlehales. **186 top:** Robert Villani; **bottom:** Jack Dermid. **187:** Jack Dermid. **188-189:** Tom Blagden, Jr. **189 top:** Joseph T. Collins/National Audubon Society Collection/PR. **190-191:** Tom Blagden, Jr. **191 top:** Steve Kaufman. **192-193 all:** Robert C. Clark. **194 left:** Wayne Lankinen/DRK Photo. **194-195:** John Tveten. **196-197 all:** Ronny Paille.

NORTHEAST

Pages 198-199: Dwight R. Kuhn. **200-201 all:** Robert Villani. **202-203:** Robert Villani. **203 top:** Johnny Johnson. **204 top:** Glenn Van Nimwegen. **204-205:** Dwight R. Kuhn. **205 right:** Dwight R. Kuhn. **206 left:** Bates Littlehales/Animals Animals. **206-207:** Dwight R. Kuhn. **207 top:** C. Gable Ray. **208-209:** Robert E. Mumford. **210-211:** Photography by Hinke/Sacilotto. **212 left:** Robert Villani; **top right:** Lynn M. Stone; **bottom right:** Robert Villani. **214-215 all:** Arthur Morris/Birds as Art. **216 left:** William S. Lea; **top right:** William S. Lea. **216-217:** Allan Sutton. **218-219 all:** William S. Lea. **220-221:** Glenn Van Nimwegen. **222-223 all:** © 1988 Lynda Richardson. **224 left:** Kjell B. Sandved. **224-225:** Glenn Van Nimwegen.

WRITERS

Bob Devine can see the Rocky Mountains from the windows of his Denver home. Formerly an associate editor and columnist for *Rocky Mountain Magazine,* he has been a freelance writer since 1982. His work has appeared in *National Geographic Traveler, Travel & Leisure, Mother Jones, Better Homes and Gardens,* and the *Boston Globe.*

Kim Heacox, a former park ranger and fisheries biologist, has lived in Alaska since 1979. He is now a freelance writer/photographer. Heacox's work has appeared in *National Geographic Traveler, Travel & Leisure, Oceans, National Wildlife,* and *International Wildlife* magazines. In 1988 he was awarded the Lowell Thomas Award for excellence in travel journalism.

Donald Dale Jackson began his career as a reporter for UPI and worked nine years as a reporter and writer for *Life.* He writes regularly for *Smithsonian, Audubon,* and *Wilderness* magazines. His books include *Gold Dust,* a history of the California gold rush, *Flying the Mail,* and *The Explorers.* He lives in Connecticut.

Laura Riley's articles and photographs have appeared in publications including *Audubon, Defenders, Ladies Home Journal, Natural History, Ranger Rick, Reader's Digest,* and *Woman's Day.* Her photos have been exhibited in numerous one-woman shows, including a nationwide tour sponsored by Eastman Kodak Company.

William Riley is a business executive and former journalist. He is co-author with his wife of *Guide to the National Wildlife Refuges* and has been active in the environmental movement in New Jersey where the Rileys reside.

Californian **Peter Steinhart** has written about natural history and environmental affairs for 17 years. His work has appeared in *Harper's, Reader's Digest,* the *New York Times,* and the *Los Angeles Times.* He is a frequent contributor to *National Wildlife* magazine and a contributing editor at *Audubon.* He is the author of *Tracks in the Sky,* a book about the Pacific flyway wildlife and wetlands.

Connie Toops' ties with nature developed during her work as a ranger at Rocky Mountain, Everglades, and other national parks. Since 1978, her writing and photography have appeared regularly in conservation publications. She has contributed to books by Time-Life and National Geographic. Her own books include *The Alligator, Birds of South Florida, The Everglades,* and *National Seashores.* She also developed the *Let's Explore* nature activity guides for children.

Joel Vance is a writer for the Missouri Department of Conservation and the author of two humor books, *Confessions of an Outdoor Maladroit* and *Grandma and the Buck Deer.* A freelance writer and president of the Outdoor Writers Association in 1989-90, he is also a columnist for four outdoor magazines.

NATIONAL WILDLIFE FEDERATION

Jay D. Hair, *President and Chief Executive Officer*

William W. Howard Jr., *Executive Vice President and Chief Operating Officer*

Alric H. Clay, *Senior Vice President, Administration*

Francis A. DiCicco, *Vice President, Financial Affairs and Treasurer*

Lynn A. Greenwalt, *Vice President and Special Assistant to the President for International Affairs*

John W. Jensen, *Vice President, Development*

S. Douglas Miller, *Vice President, Research and Education*

Kenneth S. Modzelewski, *Vice President, Promotional Activities*

Sharon L. Newsome, *Acting Vice President, Resources Conservation*

Larry J. Schweiger, *Vice President, Affiliate and Regional Programs*

Stephanie C. Sklar, *Vice President, Public Affairs*

Robert D. Strohm, *Vice President, Publications*

Joel T. Thomas, *General Counsel and Secretary*

STAFF FOR THIS BOOK

Howard Robinson, *Editorial Director*

Elaine S. Furlow, *Senior Editor*

Donna Miller, *Design Director*

Bonnie Stutski, *Photo Editor*

Michele Morris, *Research Editor*

Cei Richardson, *Editorial Assistant*

Vi Kirksey, *Editorial Secretary*

Paul Wirth, *Quality Control*

Margaret E. Wolf, *Permissions Editor*

Kathleen Furey, *Production Artist*

NATIONAL WILDLIFE FEDERATION
1400 Sixteenth Street, N.W., Washington, D.C. 20036-2266